EUROPA ⚔ MILITARIA N°39

# MILITARY PISTOLS
## HANDGUNS OF THE TWO WORLD WARS

**GORDON BRUCE**

THE CROWOOD PRESS

First published in 2016 by
The Crowood Press Ltd
Ramsbury, Marlborough
Wiltshire SN8 2HR

**www.crowood.com**

**British Library Cataloguing-in-Publication Data**
A catalogue record for this book is available from the British Library.

ISBN 978 1 78500 246 5

Typeset by Jean Cussons Typesetting, Diss, Norfolk

Printed and bound in India by Replika Press Pvt Ltd

# Contents

# Introduction

While the conventional revolver had proved itself to be a reliable weapon, the advantage of an automatic system involving a more rapid loading of more powerful ammunition seemed an inevitable choice for modern military purposes. The rifle had always been a regulation army weapon, leaving the handgun to be retained as a sidearm for personal defence in close combat situations, and a weapon of individual choice rather than one of official issue. Its use had been intended mainly for officers and non-commissioned officers. Self-loading pistols of various types were thus purchased privately by these men during World War I, but by the time of World War II they had become widely adopted by the military authorities of many nations. The armed forces of each country had selected their own preferred type of pistol with a strong emphasis on its land of origin. Competent designs of

automatic systems were prevalent throughout the early years of the twentieth century, and had been promoted by the various arms firms concerned with their manufacture. Patents were registered to protect a wide variety of methods for disengaging breech from barrel, and the loading of ammunition into the firing chamber. Systems involving the use of rotary barrels, tilting barrels and pivoting wedges had all been proposed to achieve the same result. To gain recognition and acceptance for military use, each pistol had to undergo a rigorous test programme requiring qualities of efficient operation, accuracy and reliability. Those weapons that were ultimately adopted by the authorities enabled large contracts to be awarded, together with recognition for individual designers, who have since become widely recognized throughout the world.

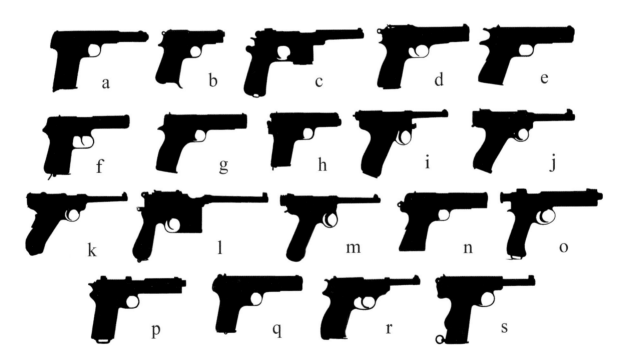

Key: A ASTRA 9mm Model 1921; B BERETTA 9mm Model 1934; C BERGMANN BAYARD 9mm Model 1910/30;
D BROWNING 9mm Model 1935; E COLT 45in Model 1911; F CZ 9mm Model 1938; G FRENCH 7.65mm Model 1935A;
H FROMMER 7.65mm Model 1911; I GLISENTI 9mm Model 1910; J LAHTI 9mm Model 1935; K LUGER 9mm Model 1908;
L MAUSER 7.63mm Model 1896; M NAMBU 8mm Model 1914; N RADOM 9mm Model 1935; O ROTH 8mm Model 1907;
P STEYR 9mm Model 1912 ; Q TOKAREV 7.62mm Model 1930; R WALTHER 9mm Model 1938 ; S WEBLEY 455in Model 1912;

# 1 Astra Model 400 (Spain)

## *Pistola de 9mm Modelo 1921 (9mm Model 1921)*

***Regulation sidearm of the Spanish military forces. Adopted by the German military in World War II***

**Factory: Unceta y Compania, Guernica, Spain**

This factory originated from the small metalwork business of Juan Esperanza and Pedro Unceta founded on 17 July 1908 at Eibar in northern Spain. Senor Unceta was a wealthy local businessman who had achieved considerable success as a manufacturer and exporter of general hardware products. The factory produced all types of metal articles, particularly as applied to the Spanish arms trade, with a large part of their business involving rifles and pistol components. Soon after the firm was established, the partners were approached by an engineer who offered them an opportunity to manufacture a novel self-loading pistol. The design was accepted and that weapon was produced in large quantities as a pocket model, enabling the factory to establish a solid financial base and create a good reputation for the quality of its products. Further opportunity for expansion presented itself in the form of a military contract to supply quantities of the Campo Giro pistol for the Spanish army in 1912. Due to the restricted working conditions at Eibar, the partners had to consider the possibility of enlarging their premises to cope with the new orders. At the town

of Guernica the local authorities were endeavouring to attract new industry to the region by offering suitable incentives.

Because of this, plus the advantage of improved rail connections in that area, it was decided to completely relocate the factory premises. In February 1913, the Esperanza y Unceta firm transferred their installation, together with all equipment, personnel and machinery, to a new site at Guernica. Management of the factory was placed under the control of Don Rufino Unceta, son of the founder, and manufacture of the Campo Giro pistol commenced almost immediately. The advent of the war in Europe imposed additional demands upon the factory to supply pistols. On 25 November 1914, the name 'Astra' was officially registered by the firm for use on their products. When Senor Esperanza retired from the firm the company title was also changed in 1926 to Unceta y Compania. The factory remained unaffected by the bombing of Guernica in the civil war of 1937, and continued to operate during World War II. In 1942, the firm was registered as a joint stock company under the title of Unceta y Compania Sociedad Anonima, and continued with the manufacture of military pistols throughout World War II. During that period, the German army purchased large numbers of arms and ammunition from the factory.

## Detail Information for the Astra Pistola de 9mm Modelo 1921

The Astra pistol was officially adopted by the Spanish Army on 6 October 1921 to supersede the regulation Model 1913 Campo Giro model. Both weapons were produced at the same factory in Guernica, with one being a direct progression of the other. The unlocked breech system and distinctive tubular breech slide were retained in the general construction, although the new

## Specifications for the Astra Pistola de 9mm Modelo 1921

**System:** Unlocked breech, blowback operated
**Calibre:** 9mm Largo
**Pistol length:** 220mm
**Barrel length:** 150mm
**Grooves:** Six RH twist
**Magazine:** Eight rounds
**Weight (empty):** 1,015g
**Weight (loaded):** 1,119g
**Safety:** Grip lever and thumb lever

pistol differed considerably in several other respects. A principal contributor to the design was Pedro Careaga, who patented several features of the weapon and who had also been involved with the development of previous models made at the factory.

Following its adoption by the army, the same model 1921 was accepted one year later for use with the Spanish police and the presidential bodyguard, after which it was manufactured commercially under the alternative title of Astra Modelo 400. The military versions had been fitted with plain wooden grip plates, while those on the commercial models were of black plastic material with a fine checkered pattern bearing the Astra Unceta factory symbol. The standard Model 400 pistol eventually gained a reputation for being capable of firing many different types of 9mm cartridge, despite its lack of a locked breech system, and a special version of the pistol was developed for the powerful parabellum round.

During World War II, the German army ordered 6,000 of

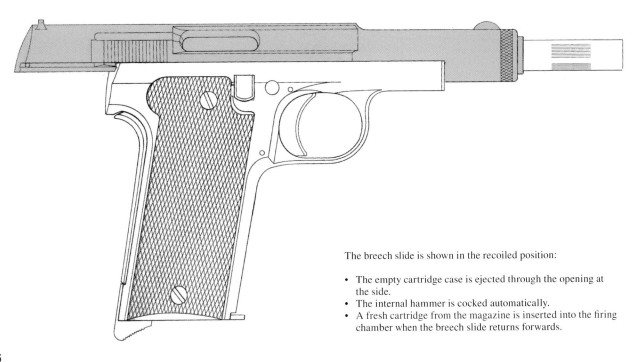

The breech slide is shown in the recoiled position:

- The empty cartridge case is ejected through the opening at the side.
- The internal hammer is cocked automatically.
- A fresh cartridge from the magazine is inserted into the firing chamber when the breech slide returns forwards.

the standard Model 400 pistols for issue to their troops stationed in occupied France. After tests had been conducted in 1943, that version was finally accepted by the German authorities as Pistole 642 (f), and duly issued to the occupation forces. The factory designation for that version was Modelo 600, and the West German police continued to be armed with it for a period after World War II. In spite of the calibre, the overall dimensions of the Model 600 were slightly less than those of the Spanish pistol.

The Astra Model 1921 does not have a locked breech, although the cartridges fired from this pistol are sometimes powerful enough to warrant such a system of operation. Constructed from top grade steel forgings, the weapon is sturdy, reliable, and finished to a high standard for its purpose as a military weapon. It was officially adopted as a sidearm for all Spanish army, navy, air force, police and prison services.

**The breech slide:** Cylindrical and contains the barrel, recoil spring, extractor and firing pin, the latter being fired by a concealed hammer located within the pistol body. An opening at the right side of the breech slide allows spent cartridge cases to be ejected as the weapon is fired.

**The recoil spring:** Surrounds the barrel and is sufficiently strong to withstand the recoil from most discharges. It is held within the breech slide by a tubular collar at the front end, where it is secured by a knurled muzzle ring. Removal of the ring permits the weapon to be dismantled for routine maintenance.

**The magazine:** Inserted from beneath the grip and retained by a catch at the lower back end of the grip. In the event of a live round remaining in the firing chamber, trigger action is blocked when the magazine is withdrawn and cannot be activated.

**Safety lever:** Positioned at the left side of the pistol body and operated by thumb action to engage a locking notch in the breech slide. A hinged lever at the back of the grip automatically disconnects the firing mechanism and only permits the weapon to be fired when correctly depressed by hand.

**Grip plates:** Normally of wood cut with a fine chequered pattern on the surface. Each plate is secured to the pistol body by a screw at the top and another at the base. An opening at the lower rear end of the left-hand plate surrounds a fixed lanyard ring.

**Cartridge Information**
Details for the 9mm Largo cartridge:

**Bullet weight:** 8.5g
**Bullet diameter:** 9.02mm
**Bullet length:** 16.1mm
**Case length:** 22.8mm
**Rim diameter:** 9.96mm
**Cartridge length:** 33.5mm
**Cartridge weight:** 13g
**Initial velocity:** 365m/s

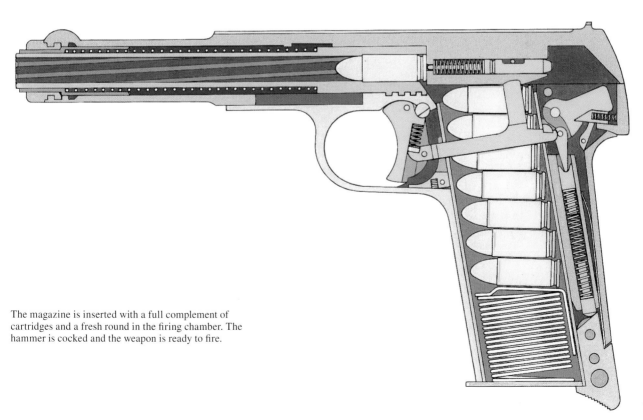

The magazine is inserted with a full complement of cartridges and a fresh round in the firing chamber. The hammer is cocked and the weapon is ready to fire.

# 2 Beretta Model 1934 (Italy)

## *Pistola Modella 934 9mm Corto (9mm Model 1934)*

*Regulation sidearm of the Italian military forces. Adopted by the German military in World War II*

**Factory: Fabbrica d'Armi Pietro Beretta, Gardone, Italy**

The Italian Beretta firm was originally founded in the year 1680 by thirty-year-old Pietro Beretta of Lodovico, who opened a small workshop in Gardone to make gun barrels for pistols and muzzle loaders. Situated in the Trompia valley some 10 miles north of Brescia, the region had been a centre for gunsmiths and armourers for centuries. Workmen employed by Beretta became predominant among other artisans of the region, and earned a reputation for the high quality of their product. On the death of Pietro Beretta, his factory was taken over by the eldest of his eight sons, who ultimately passed the business on to his own heir. In that manner, the firm remained in the family for many generations. By the mid-nineteenth century, the management had been inherited by Pier Guiseppe Beretta, who controlled the business for over thirty years. He travelled extensively during that period, not only

throughout Italy but also abroad to promote a wider interest in the factory products. At the Esposizione Bresciana of 1857 the Beretta firm displayed a wide and comprehensive range of arms, including sabres, daggers, lances, rifles and pistols. It was then the sole representative of the local arms industry, and evoked considerable interest at a time when the region remained under the yoke of Austrian domination.

After the unification of Italy in 1870, the new imperial armies were supplied with large quantities of firearms from the Gardone factory. Meanwhile the Beretta hunting arms had regained their popularity, and so Pier Guiseppe decided to combine all aspects of their manufacture under a single roof. A new building occupying an area of approximately 1,000 square metres was erected in 1880, and the plant was completely refurbished with modern tools and machinery. Hydro-electric power was installed, and fresh methods in organization were adopted.

After the death of Pier Guiseppe in 1903, leadership of the Beretta concern was transferred to Pietro, the eldest of his five sons, who continued to implement the programme of expansion started by his father. Born in April 1870 and holder of the award Cavaliere dell Corona d'Italia, Pietro brought a new and important phase of development to the history of the Beretta plant. Under his guidance, the production of arms was even further increased as a result of his wide experience of foreign mass-production techniques, which he utilized to great effect. Prior to May 1915 their chief product had been shotguns, but the advent of war caused the entire plant to meet a demand for military weapons, and a new range of automatic arms materialized.

## Specifications for the Beretta Pistola Modella 934 9mm Corto

**System:** Unlocked breech, blowback operated
**Calibre:** 9mm Short
**Pistol length:** 150mm
**Barrel length:** 88mm
**Grooves:** Six RH twist
**Magazine:** Seven rounds
**Weight (empty):** 625g
**Weight (loaded):** 692g
**Safety:** Thumb lever

## Detail Information for the Beretta Pistola Modella 934 9mm Corto

The 1934 model was developed from an earlier Model 1915 Beretta pistol, both of which were created by Tullio Maregoni, chief designer at the factory. It had been introduced at the request of the Italian government to supersede the current Glisenti Model 1910, which employed a slightly more powerful cartridge than the 9mm Corto, and featured a semi-locked breech system. The new Beretta was first used in action by the Italian army during the war between Italy and Ethiopia in 1935, and was subsequently issued as standard equipment for the Italian contingent supporting General Franco throughout the Spanish Civil War of the late 1930s. In the

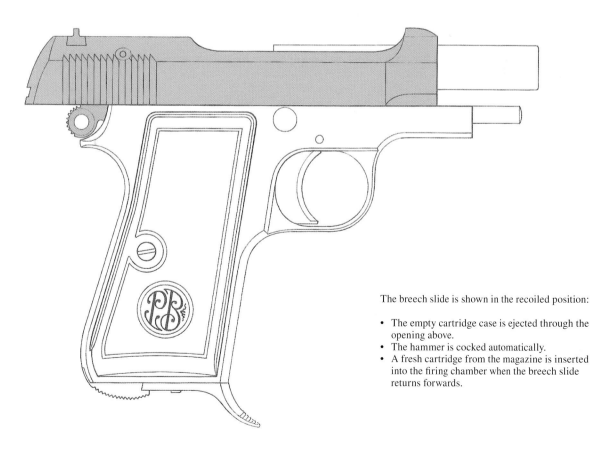

The breech slide is shown in the recoiled position:

- The empty cartridge case is ejected through the opening above.
- The hammer is cocked automatically.
- A fresh cartridge from the magazine is inserted into the firing chamber when the breech slide returns forwards.

long period of world conflict that followed these events the Beretta pistol was used extensively during the campaigns in Europe and North Africa, where it proved to be a rugged and reliable sidearm of excellent design requiring a minimum of maintenance.

Pistols issued to the Italian army were identified with a crown over the initials RE (Regio Escercito), while those issued to the air force were marked with an eagle symbol. A police version of the weapon, chambered for a 7.65mm cartridge, was introduced in 1935 and manufactured for the commercial market as the Model 935. That version was eventually also adopted by the Italian air force and identified with the initials RA (Regio Aeronautica) or AM (Aeronautica Militare). Beretta pistols supplied to the navy carried the letters RM (Regio Marina), while those for the police were marked PS (Pubblica Sicurezza).

During World War II the 1934 model, like so many other national weapons, was absorbed into German military equipment as the Pistole 671 (i). The original pistol still remained as a regulation Italian sidearm until 1951, when it was replaced by another Beretta pistol featuring a locked breech. The model 934 has since become one of the most famous of all Italian handguns.

The design of this weapon is both simple and ingenious. It does not have a locked breech system because of the slightly lower power of its 9mm Short cartridge. Components in the assembly are reduced to a functional minimum, with some items performing more than one operation. Although the barrel is fixed rigidly to the pistol body it is readily detachable. A lug projecting from beneath the chamber end fits into a hole at the top of the pistol body, where it is retained by the stem of the safety lever.

**The breech slide:** Contains the extractor and firing pin, and has appropriately inclined surfaces on its interior to facilitate the installation and removal of the barrel. For the same purpose, a major part of its length is open at the upper surface and is a feature that also allows for maximum cooling of the barrel during repeated firing.

**The recoil spring:** Positioned beneath the barrel and has a solid central guide rod. When the weapon is fired, the rod is allowed to protrude through the front of the pistol body.

**The grip plates:** Of moulded plastic with a steel backing, each retained by a single screw. Central areas of the plates are stippled to provide a non-slip surface.

**The safety lever:** Mounted at the left side of the pistol body directly above the trigger. Rotating it to the rear locks the trigger and exposes a green dot to indicate that the weapon is on 'Safe'. It also engages a notch under the breech slide to hold it in position.

**The magazine:** Retained in position by a spring-operated catch at the lower rear end of the grip. The magazine base plate has an extension at the front to accommodate a large-handed shooter. A lanyard swivel is attached at the lower rear side.

**The firing mechanism:** Achieved by an external hammer striking the firing pin.

### Cartridge Information
Details for the 9mm Short cartridge:

**Bullet weight:** 6.15g
**Bullet diameter:** 9.03mm
**Bullet length:** 11.3mm
**Case length:** 17.27mm
**Rim diameter:** 9.5mm
**Cartridge length:** 25mm
**Cartridge weight:** 9.55g
**Initial velocity:** 270m/s

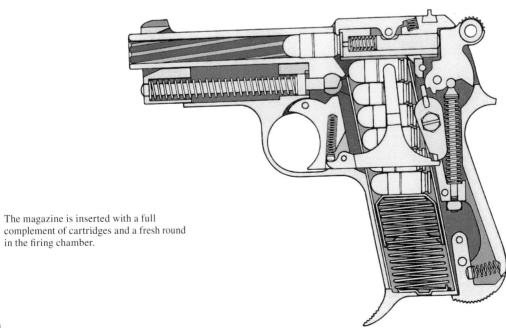

The magazine is inserted with a full complement of cartridges and a fresh round in the firing chamber.

# 3 Bergmann-Bayard Model 1910/21 (Denmark)

## *Bergmann 9mm Modele 1910/21 (9mm Model 1910)*

### *Regulation sidearm of the Danish military forces in both World Wars*

**Factory: Anciens Établissements Pieper, Liège, Belgium**

Anciens Établissements Pieper was formed as a limited company in 1905 for the manufacture of patented automatic firearms, cycles and ammunition. The original business, known simply as Henri Pieper Arms manufacturer, had been founded in 1866. Pieper was the holder of many firearms patents, which featured improvements to pistols, rifles and ammunition. At various international exhibitions he had received several awards for his contributions to the development of weapons. In order to achieve the output of military and civil weapons he had engaged the services of no fewer than 1,500 workers, many of whom were employed in small workshops in the vicinity of Liège. Relatively few of the local factories were then capable of manufacturing complete weapons on a large scale, and most of the work had to be subcontracted to individual specialists. Pieper decided to reorganize the whole process on a mass-production basis, using modern machinery within his own factory. He had acquired premises on the Rue des Bayards in Liège, where he installed the latest machinery

and new machine tools, some of which he had designed himself. Because of his more efficient methods of production, he was then able to guarantee a rapid delivery of weapons to several foreign countries.

Following the death of Henri Pieper in 1898 the entire concern was administered by his son Nicholas, who had already been closely involved in the factory management. Further designs of new weapons played an important role in the development of the firm after the turn of the century, and more honours were awarded at trade fairs held throughout Europe. In 1905, the factory was re-formed under a new trading name of Anciens Établissements Pieper, and in the following year it commenced production of a novel self-loading pistol patented by Nicholas Pieper. At that time a licence had been obtained from the German firm of Eisenwerke Gaggenau for the manufacture of a Bergmann military pistol to be supplied to the Spanish government. When the German army invaded Belgium in 1914, however, the factory was ordered to cease all production of pistols, although manufacture was resumed after 1918 with improved versions of earlier models. Further expansion of the Pieper enterprise was severely restricted by the financial crisis, and the firm was on the verge of collapse when a large order for sub-machineguns was received in 1934 from the Belgian army. Production of the Bergmann pistol continued until a second German invasion seized control of the factory in 1940.

## Detail Information for the Bergmann-Bayard 9mm Modele 1910/21

The Bergmann-Bayard model 1910 pistol was adopted by the Danish army on 22 September 1911, and remained in service for nearly twenty-seven years. It was then the first automatic pistol to be accepted by that country. It had been developed from a succes-

## Specifications for the Bergmann-Bayard 9mm Model 1910/21

**System:** Locked breech, recoil operated
**Calibre:** 9mm Bayard Long
**Pistol length:** 250mm
**Barrel length:** 102mm
**Grooves:** Six LH twist
**Magazine:** Six rounds
**Weight (empty):** 1,000g
**Weight (loaded):** 1,075g
**Safety:** Thumb lever

sion of earlier models in various calibres that were designed and manufactured at the Bergmann Industriewerke in Germany. They were the first truly successful blowback-operated handguns, and had embodied original features patented by a Hungarian Otto Brauswetter, with later improvements by Hugo Schmeisser, culminating in the model of 1910. After production had been taken over by the Belgian AEP firm, firing trials of the latest design were conducted by the Danish military arms commission, who approved the weapon for service use. It also underwent testing by the British War Office in 1910 but was rejected because of its calibre.

The Pieper factory produced nearly 5,000 of these pistols before World War I, when the German invasion of Belgium brought an abrupt halt to further deliveries. During the initial period of occupation, another 1,000 pistols were produced at Liège for issue to local police organizations. Commercial manufacture then continued after the war using surplus components

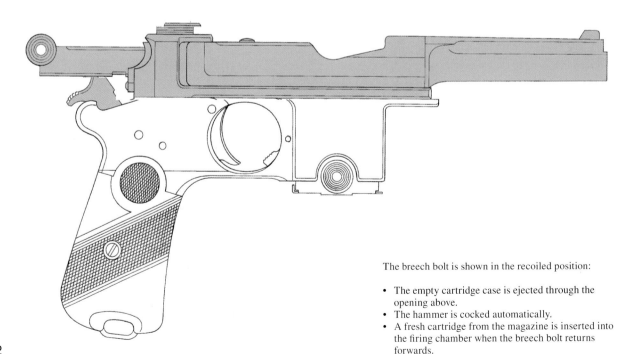

The breech bolt is shown in the recoiled position:

- The empty cartridge case is ejected through the opening above.
- The hammer is cocked automatically.
- A fresh cartridge from the magazine is inserted into the firing chamber when the breech bolt returns forwards.

from earlier manufacture. By 1922, the Danes had commenced their own manufacture of the 1910 model at the Royal Arsenal in Copenhagen for the Danish army. It remained in service as a regulation sidearm until the German invasion of World War II, after which the factory was seized by the Wehrmacht. During the occupation, the Bergmann pistol was re-classified by the Germans as Pistole 644(d) and issued to units stationed in Denmark. While the 1910 model was still officially the service pistol of the Danish army during the war, it was eventually withdrawn from further use in 1945.

Designed as a short recoil, locked breech pistol, the Bergmann-Bayard model originally featured a barrel that screwed into an extension, which continued to the rear over the entire upper part of the pistol body. In the current version, the barrel has been incorporated as an integral part of the extension, and a separate breech bolt is held within the rear portion by means of a hollow locking block. Locking is achieved by the block engaging with two grooves formed on the underside of the bolt so that when it recoils after firing, the block is cammed downwards, out of the grooves, into a recess on the pistol body, leaving the breech bolt free to continue moving back.

**The breech bolt:** Rectangular in section and contains an extractor at the front end, plus a long firing pin with its spring held in place by a solid cross bolt at the rear. A small diameter recoil spring is also positioned around the firing pin, which serves as its guide.

**The firing mechanism:** A basic single-action revolver style with an external hammer. The lockwork is accessible via a removable coverplate attached to the right-hand side of the pistol body by a spring-loaded plunger, and released by pressing a button that is recessed at the opposite side of the weapon.

**The safety lever:** Positioned at the left rear side of the pistol body, where it can be rotated to lock the hammer in either a cocked or a non-cocked setting.

**The magazine:** Located ahead of the trigger and retained in place by a spring-loaded catch accessible from within the trigger guard. It contains the cartridges in two compact vertical rows.

**The grip plates:** Originally of wood, with both held to the grip portion by a single screw at the right-hand side of the pistol. These were later replaced by plates of a black synthetic Trolit material. Provision is made at the butt base for the attachment of a lanyard.

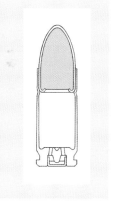

**Cartridge Information**
Details for the 9mm Bayard Long cartridge:

**Bullet weight:** 8.3g
**Bullet diameter:** 9.02mm
**Bullet length:** 16mm
**Case length:** 23mm
**Rim diameter:** 9.65mm
**Cartridge length:** 33.5mm
**Cartridge weight:** 12.75g
**Initial velocity:** 360 m/s

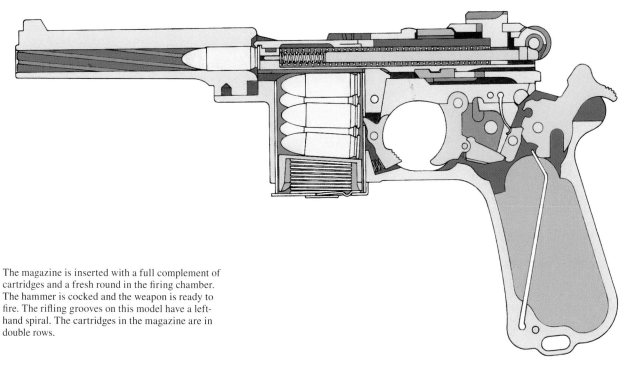

The magazine is inserted with a full complement of cartridges and a fresh round in the firing chamber. The hammer is cocked and the weapon is ready to fire. The rifling grooves on this model have a left-hand spiral. The cartridges in the magazine are in double rows.

# 4 Browning Model 1935 (Belgium)

## *Pistolet Modele 1935 Grande Puissance (9mm Model 1935)*

*Regulation sidearm of the Belgian military forces in World War II*

**Factory: Fabrique Nationale d'Armes
de Guerre, Herstal, Belgium**

The Belgian National Arms factory was formed on 3 July 1889 by a syndicate composed of Belgian gunmakers, amongst whom were such names as Henri Pieper, Émile and Léon Nagant, Pirlot and Fresart, August Francotte and others, with financial backing obtained from Crédit Général Liégeois SA and Nicolas Vivario. In addition, the Belgian government had participated to the extent of a guaranteed order for 150,000 Mauser rifles. The factory was located at Herstal in Liège Province, a region that had been actively involved in the manufacture of weapons since the Middle Ages. After the rifle contract had been fulfilled, certain legal problems occurred with the Mauser firm, as a result of which half of the stock shares were acquired by the Ludwig Leowe firm in Germany. After a brief period of inactivity in the manufacture of arms, a meeting with John Browning, the inventor of a new self-loading pistol, brought renewed life to the factory when

it obtained the exclusive rights for this pistol's manufacture in Europe. An agreement to that effect was signed on 17 July 1897, enabling the Belgian firm to develop the weapon commercially and thereby setting into motion a long and profitable association with the American inventor, who contributed so much to the success of the factory.

Throughout the early years of the twentieth century the factory also undertook production of the Browning automatic shotgun, many of which were exported to the United States. By 1910 another Browning pistol design was being produced and supplied to various nations as an official police weapon. When the factory was captured by German forces in August 1914, all production machinery was confiscated and the plant became inoperative, until the Germans took over the premises three years later and installed a repair centre for army vehicles.

At the end of World War I the firm became a wholly Belgian-owned concern for the manufacture of pistols and shotguns. Output was resumed, and continued during the post-war period with nearly 11,000 workers employed at the Herstal plant. Shortly after the invasion of Belgium in May 1940, many of the engineers and technicians had escaped abroad, where they continued their work on the manufacture of Browning pistols. Meanwhile, the factory with all its equipment had been seized by the occupation forces and placed under the direction of the German Arms factory in Berlin. Additional technicians were then transferred from that plant to operate the factory under German supervision.

## Detail Information for the Browning 9mm Modele Grande Puissance

The Browning 9mm Modele Grande Puissance was adopted by the army of Belgium in 1935 as their official military sidearm. The weapon was originally created by John Browning in response to

## Specifications for the Browning Pistolet Modele 1935 Grande Puissance

**System:** Locked breech, recoil operated
**Calibre:** 9mm
**Pistol length:** 197mm
**Barrel length:** 118mm
**Grooves:** Six RH twist
**Magazine:** Thirteen rounds
**Weight (empty):** 900g
**Weight (loaded):** 1,060g
**Safety:** Thumb lever

the French government requirement for a new service pistol with an extra-large magazine capacity. The design was first created in 1923, and subsequently patented in the United States and other countries. It was the third Browning locked-breech pistol design to reach manufacturing stage, the others being a model 1900 and model 1911, both produced by the Colt firm. Production of the High Power model took place at the Belgian FN factory in Liège prior to World War II. There were two distinct versions: the standard pattern had fixed sights and was issued with a conventional holster, while the other had an adjustable rear sight and featured a detachable wooden shoulder stock.

In 1938 the pistol was approved by the Rumanian government, and in the following year Denmark, China, Esthonia and Peru each accepted the design, although the German invasion of Belgium in 1940 prevented deliveries being made. Production was continued under the control of the occupation forces, and the weapon then used extensively by the Germans as Pistole 640 (b). By the end of the war, approximately 319,000 had been produced

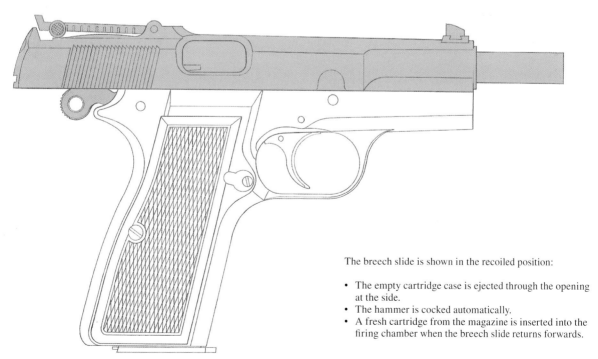

The breech slide is shown in the recoiled position:

- The empty cartridge case is ejected through the opening at the side.
- The hammer is cocked automatically.
- A fresh cartridge from the magazine is inserted into the firing chamber when the breech slide returns forwards.

in that manner. Two versions of the pistol were also manufactured by the John Inglis factory in Canada between 1943 and 1945, when a total of over 151,000 were produced for Great Britain and the Allies. The Canadian company introduced a number of modifications to the mechanism, and also offered the weapon in various presentation forms. A gold-plated example with white grip plates was constructed for the Canadian Prime Minister, and another for the President of Mexico. The Browning High Power model 1935 is one of the most widely distributed pistols in the world.

As its title suggests, the Browning High Power model is chambered for the powerful 9mm Parabellum cartridge, and employs a locked breech system constructed along similar lines to the Colt M1911, in which the barrel is held to the breech slide by two ribs engaging two recesses. In place of a swinging link, as on the Colt, the method of disengagement is accomplished through a cammed lug acting on a stop within the pistol body to lower the barrel as it recoils when the weapon is fired. It features a short recoil system in which the barrel remains locked with the recoiling breech for a brief period before being disconnected.

**The breech slide assembly:** Contains the firing pin and extractor. An opening at the right-hand side of the breech slide allows spent cartridge cases to be ejected after firing.

**The recoil spring:** Lies beneath the barrel in a channel on the pistol body, where it is guided by a long pin at its rear. A smaller secondary spring is contained within the guide pin to increase tension against the slide stop pin.

**The magazine:** A removable box containing thirteen rounds, and held in position by a spring-loaded catch passing through the pistol body. Depressing the catch at the left-hand side of the grip permits the magazine to be withdrawn. The trigger is then unable to operate the firing mechanism until the magazine is returned.

**A safety lever:** Positioned at the upper rear side of the grip, it can be moved upwards to obstruct the sear and lock the hammer. It also engages one of the notches under the breech slide to retain it in either the closed or open position.

**The grip plates:** These are of walnut with a central chequered pattern; each is secured to the pistol body by a single screw at the rear.

**The firing mechanism:** Consists of an external hammer and internal firing pin.

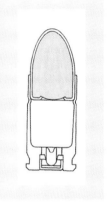

**Cartridge Information**
Details for the 9mm Parabellum cartridge:

**Bullet weight:** 8g
**Bullet diameter:** 9.02mm
**Bullet length:** 15.1mm
**Case length:** 19mm
**Rim diameter:** 10mm
**Cartridge length:** 28.85mm
**Cartridge weight:** 12.1g
**Initial velocity:** 345m/s

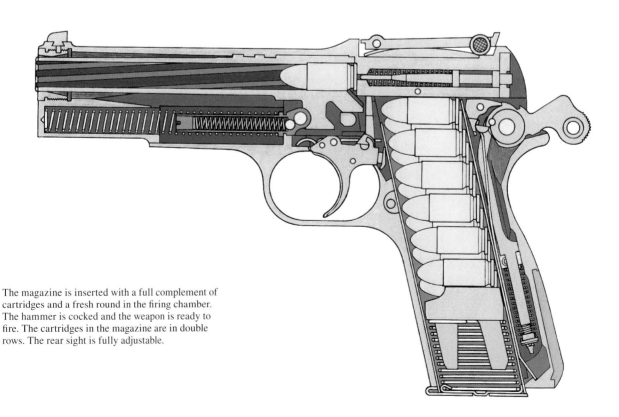

The magazine is inserted with a full complement of cartridges and a fresh round in the firing chamber. The hammer is cocked and the weapon is ready to fire. The cartridges in the magazine are in double rows. The rear sight is fully adjustable.

# 5  Colt Model 1911 (USA)

## Colt Government Model 1911A1 (.45 Model 1911)

*Regulation sidearm of the American military forces in both World Wars*

**Factory: Colt's Patent Firearms Manufacturing Company, Hartford, Connecticut, USA**

On 5 August 1835, the Patent Arms Manufacturing Company was established by Samuel Colt in Paterson, New Jersey, USA with backing supplied by several New York financiers. Colt himself was in charge of sales promotion, and from the outset it had been his firm intention to gain a significant contract from the government for the large-scale manufacture of revolvers. The company was then primarily engaged in the production of ring lever rifles, and in spite of securing a number of contracts from various state militia, their sales had not proved sufficient for the enterprise to remain viable. Internal friction among the investors added to the gradual collapse, and by December 1842 the business was liquidated.

An outbreak of war between the United States and Mexico in 1846 encouraged Colt to direct his talents once more to designing weapons. Orders were soon received for a supply of revolvers for the US cavalry, and this enabled him to set up his own manufacturing plant in Hartford, Connecticut; for the next eight years

the new factory maintained a virtual monopoly on the production of those weapons. In 1867 the Colt Company also became responsible for the production of the Gatling machinegun, several hundreds of which were supplied to imperial Russia.

The advent of the famous Peacemaker model of 1871 brought further success for the factory, and several thousands of these revolvers were purchased by the US Ordnance Department between 1873 and 1891. By 1900 the factory had commenced manufacture of a new automatic pistol design based on the patents of John Browning, and introduced the first pistol of that type to be manufactured in the USA. This was followed by a series of other developments, culminating in the adoption of a calibre 45 model in 1911 as a result of official tests by the military authorities. From 1917 until the end of World War I, production of these weapons at the Colt plant had reached a total of 435,500, while similar quantities were manufactured at other plants in the USA. In the summer of 1920 a contract was obtained for the manufacture of 15,000 Thompson sub-machineguns, many of which were maintained as law enforcement weapons during the Prohibition era. In addition to orders from the army, by the year 1934 the police departments of more than 400 cities in the United States had also adopted Colt revolvers. Throughout World War II almost 1,900,000 Colt pistols were supplied to the United States military from various factories involved in their manufacture.

## Detail Information for the Colt 45 Model 1911A1

The creation of an American automatic handgun originated with a patent of 1897 and led to a series of pistols produced by the Colt factory, culminating with a military model of 1911. This version of the famous Colt 45 military automatic pistol was adopted for

### Specifications for the Colt Government Model 1911A1

**System:** Locked breech, recoil operated
**Calibre:** 11.4mm
**Pistol length:** 216mm
**Barrel length:** 127mm
**Grooves:** Six LH twist
**Magazine:** Seven rounds
**Weight (empty):** 1,106g
**Weight (loaded):** 1,254g
**Safety:** Thumb lever and grip lever

service with the United States Army on 15 June 1926, superseding the previous Colt model of 1911. It was designed and patented by John Browning, who had already been responsible for the creation of several previous Colt automatic pistols. The new 1911A1 version was an improvement on its predecessor in that it incorporated various modifications required by the government. This version has since become renowned for its robust qualities as a service weapon used by the US army throughout the two World Wars.

In earlier tests conducted by the US Ordnance Department it had been decreed that nothing less than a 45 calibre would be considered suitable for military purposes. Extensive trials were also undertaken by the British War Office, who reached a similar conclusion, although they decided not to adopt the weapon as an official service handgun. The Americans were far more positive and accepted the Colt 45 as a regulation arm for all branches of

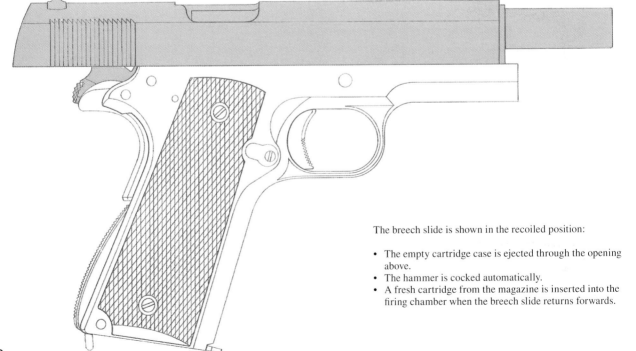

The breech slide is shown in the recoiled position:

- The empty cartridge case is ejected through the opening above.
- The hammer is cocked automatically.
- A fresh cartridge from the magazine is inserted into the firing chamber when the breech slide returns forwards.

the army, air force, navy and marine corps. Orders to supply the pistol were also received from the Norwegian government and from the Republic of Argentina. During World War I, the Colt factory produced no fewer than 425,500 of the 1911 model, but by far the highest rate of manufacture occurred during World War II, when approximately 520,000 of the A1 version were produced for the United States government. In addition to the Colt factory, various other gun manufacturers were involved at that period, as a result of which the grand total eventually reached nearly 2,000,000.

Limited quantities of the pistol were later supplied to the British government in order to supplement the standard pistols issued to all branches of their armed forces. In wartime, as with so many foreign weapons seized by the Germans, the Colt 45 model was given its own specific title of Pistole 660(a), although the large calibre would have been quite unsuitable for use by the enemy, who were devoted to 9mm.

**The barrel:** In the government model it is held within the breech slide, with a barrel bushing at the front; it is provided with two ribs on the upper surface that engage with two corresponding slots on the inner surface of the breech slide. A pivoted link is attached to a lug projecting from beneath the lower rear end of the barrel, and is also connected to a stop pin through the pistol body. This enables the barrel to disconnect automatically from the breech as the latter recoils on firing. The hammer is then cocked automatically.

**The breech slide assembly:** Contains the extractor, firing pin and spring. There are two notches cut into the left-hand side into which the safety lock can be engaged to hold the breech in either an open or closed position.

**The recoil spring:** Located in an open channel on the pistol body, where it is compressed between a long tubular plug at the front and a tubular spring guide rod at the rear.

**The magazine:** Held in place by a catch at the left side of the grip, from where it can be depressed by thumb to release it.

**The safety lever:** Positioned at the left side of the pistol body; it can be moved upwards to engage a notch in the breech slide when the hammer is cocked, and locks the firing mechanism. There is also a grip safety feature at the rear of the grip to prevent the weapon from being fired until it is held correctly in the hand.

**The grip plates:** Of walnut, with the entire outer surface cut with a chequered pattern. Each plate is secured to the grip by a screw at the top and another at the lower end.

**Cartridge Information**
Details for the .45in Colt cartridge:

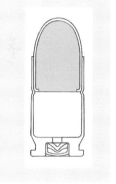

**Bullet weight:** 14.9g
**Bullet diameter:** 11.5mm
**Bullet length:** 17.3mm
**Case length:** 22.8mm
**Rim diameter:** 12mm
**Cartridge length:** 29.8mm
**Cartridge weight:** 21.2g
**Initial velocity:** 259m/s

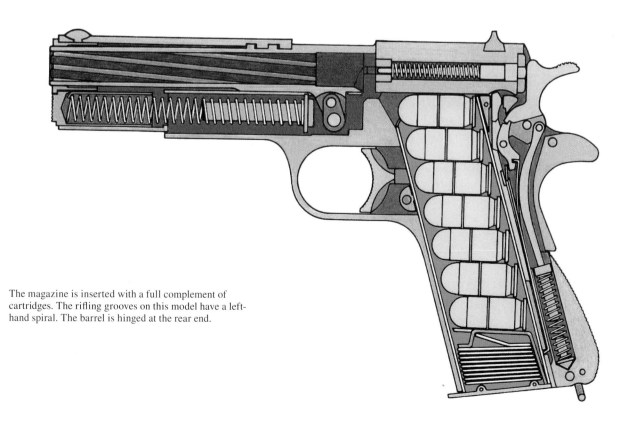

The magazine is inserted with a full complement of cartridges. The rifling grooves on this model have a left-hand spiral. The barrel is hinged at the rear end.

# 6  CZ Model 1938 (Czechoslovakia)

## *Armadni Pistole Vzor 38 (9mm Model 1938)*

### *Regulation sidearm of the Czechoslovakian military forces in World War II*

**Factory: Česká Zbrojovka, Strakonice, Czechoslovakia**

A foundation firm of Česká Zbrojovka had been established originally as Jihoceska Zbrojovka of Plzen, Bohemia, in 1919, by a Czechoslovakian architect named Karel Bubla. Bubla had obtained support from three directors of the Skoda firm, Messrs Hanus, Hasek and Havranek, in an effort to avoid the necessity of importing large quantities of arms from abroad. Financial control was retained by the Trade and Industry Bank of Plzen, and the factory placed under the management of the Czech gunsmith, Alois Tomiska. It was he who had designed the first pistol to be produced at the factory in the years 1919 to 1921.

The original location of the factory was at rented premises known as Habelmayer Mill in Plzen, where the pistol was produced until 1921; the entire workforce was then relocated to a new factory building at Strakonice under the supervision of a Skoda works engineer named Bartsch. In 1922, the firm merged with the Hubertus factory and altered its trading name to Česká Zbrojovka akciova spolecnost. Within the next two years other branch factories were opened in Prague and at Uhersky Brod in eastern Moravia, although the main factory remained at Strakonice for the exclusive manufacture of pistols.

The Ministerstvo Narodni Obrany had assigned a commission to report on the facilities available for the mass production of military arms in Czechoslovakia. As a result of their findings, the manufacture of rifles and machineguns was concentrated at Ceskoslovenska Zbrojovka in Brno, and their pistol production transferred to Strakonice in 1923; Česká Zbrojovka was the largest pistol manufacturer in the country, producing weapons for the police and military authorities on a large scale, as well as many being exported to several countries through the world. In spite of the previous decision, machineguns built under special licence from the British firms of Vickers and Lewis were also produced at Strakonice during the following years. Included with those weapons were signal pistols and repeating air rifles designed for training purposes.

By the year 1928, the manufacture of bicycles and motorcycles had been included at the factory. Between 1937 and 1938 production commenced of a pistol and new machinegun for the Czech army, although very few were constructed before the country was overtaken by war. On 1 October 1939 German troops entered Sudetenland, and by March 1940 the factory was under the control of the German army.

## Detail Information for the CZ Vzor 1938 9mm Armadni Pistole

Czechoslovakia has produced many fine pistols in the past, but it was not until 1937 that the Ministry of National Defence proposed that a new 9mm pistol should be designed and manufactured in that country specially for the army. The project was undertaken by Frantisek Myska, an engineer at the Strakonice factory who had been involved with the design of earlier models. As it had been decided that the particular 9mm cartridge for service use would

**Specifications for the Armadni Pistole Vzor 38**
**System:** Unlocked breech, blowback operated
**Calibre:** 9mm Short
**Pistol length:** 197mm
**Barrel length:** 118mm
**Grooves:** Six RH twist
**Magazine:** Eight rounds
**Weight (empty):** 923g
**Weight (loaded):** 1,000g
**Safety:** None

not require the complicated locked breech system of previously used foreign pistols, Myska designed a hinged barrel arrangement that was patented in November 1936. Prototypes were then constructed in which various safety devices were included, and the pistols subjected to a programme of field testing by the military authorities. Interest in the new pistol at that time was expressed by the Rumanian Purchasing Committee.

During the various firing trials that were conducted, cavalry officers had insisted on a pistol where the hammer did not remain cocked after firing. Consequently, the new pistol featured a double-action trigger mechanism, which also dispensed with a safety device. The pistol was officially introduced to the Czechoslovakian armed forces on 1 June 1938 by a circular from the Chief of General Staff, and the Ministry of National Defence later ordered 41,000 of the new pistols. Although production had commenced in that year, very few of the weapons were produced for the military before the factory was taken over by the German

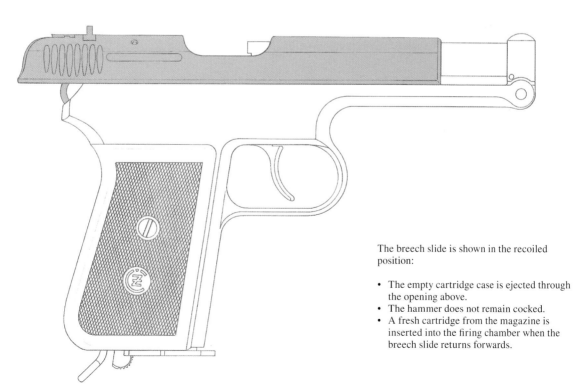

The breech slide is shown in the recoiled position:

- The empty cartridge case is ejected through the opening above.
- The hammer does not remain cocked.
- A fresh cartridge from the magazine is inserted into the firing chamber when the breech slide returns forwards.

army. Limited manufacture of the CZ38 pistol still continued during the occupation, but as the weapon had not been designed to shoot the German service Parabellum round, it was not adopted to the same extent as the handguns of other occupied nations. Given its requisition title of P39 (t), it was used only as a supplementary pistol for the Todt organization, the police and local officials.

This weapon was specially designed to be simple, safe to operate, and easy to maintain. The breech is unlocked at the point of firing and operates solely on a blowback principle, while the firing mechanism is similar to that of a double-action revolver, where the hammer is cocked only by the trigger. Some prototype versions were given a slightly different contour at the rear of the breech to permit access to the hammer for it to be cocked by hand. At the same time, a manually operated safety device had been proposed to lock the cocked hammer, but this was soon considered to be unnecessary and it was then eliminated from future production. A magazine safety feature had also been fitted to some earlier models, but this was dispensed with for similar reasons, thus keeping the weapon basically simple for service use.

**The breech slide:** Contains the extractor, firing pin and its spring. The firing pin is retained by a sliding cover at the rear of the breech and is readily accessible. Removal of the breech slide and access to the barrel is achieved conveniently by moving a sliding catch at the left side of the pistol body.

**The barrel:** Attached at the front to a hinged collar, which allows it to be swung forwards for routine maintenance.

**The recoil spring:** Lies in a hollow beneath and parallel to the barrel, with spring guides at both the front and rear ends.

**The grip plates:** Of wood with a chequered pattern, and formed as a single piece secured to the pistol body by a screw at each side.

**The magazine:** Retained by a spring catch at the lower rear end of the grip, where it is surrounded by a lanyard loop.

**The firing mechanism:** Allows the hammer to be cocked only by trigger action, and is covered by a detachable side plate at the left side of the pistol body. This provides an excellent arrangement for inspection and maintenance to the lockwork.

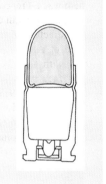

**Cartridge Information**
Details for the 9mm Short cartridge:

**Bullet weight:** 6.15g
**Bullet diameter:** 9.03mm
**Bullet length:** 11.3mm
**Case length:** 17.27mm
**Rim diameter:** 9.5mm
**Cartridge length:** 25mm
**Cartridge weight:** 9.55g
**Initial velocity:** 270m/s

The magazine is inserted with a full complement of cartridges. The barrel is hinged to the front end of the pistol.

# 7 French Model 1935A (France)

## *Pistolet Automatique Modèle 1935A (7.65mm Model 1935A)*

*Regulation sidearm of the French military forces in World War II*

**Factory: Société Alsacienne de Constructions Mécaniques, Cholet, France**

The company was formed in 1872 after a merger between two mechanical engineering firms, Bock, Koechlin et Thierry, and the Société de Graffenstaden of Alsace. The founder of the original firm was a French industrialist named André Koechlin, who established his main engineering works at Mulhouse in 1826 for the manufacture of textile machinery and steam engines under the title of André Koechlin et Compagnie. After the amalgamation with the Graffenstaden society the new firm created another factory at Belfort, which subsequently became a separate company in 1913; from the beginning of World War I, the factory was placed under German control. In 1921, the Société Alsacienne de Constructions Mécaniques (SACM) became the French Limited Company; two years later it was reunited with the Belfort factory, with its head office at No 1 Rue de la Fonderie in Mulhouse, and a branch office at No 32 Rue de Lisbonne in Paris. Following an association with gun designer Charles Petter, in 1934 another factory was established at Cholet – in the Maine

et Loire department and approximately 50km from Nantes in north-west France – to exploit his designs for the manufacture of military and police weapons.

The site on which the factory was erected covered a fairly large area that had formerly been occupied by a Pellamail factory laundry. The first director of the Cholet plant was a Monsieur Maud, and between the years 1935 and 1939 the factory produced pistols and other armaments. In addition to the 1935A Petter model, these included a prototype sub-machinegun known as the Pistolet Mitrailleur Modele 1939, also designed by Charles Petter, and officially adopted by the French government in October of that year. Unfortunately that weapon was never constructed in time for delivery to the army before the fall of France in World War II: the factory was taken over by the Germans on 20 June 1940, with all further production of arms placed under their supervision.

At the end of the war the factory remained in operation and continued to expand, with another branch being erected at Mulhouse. During the 1950s, however, the business gradually declined, and by 1957 the Cholet plant was abandoned, with all buildings, material and land being divided amongst various companies of the locality. In 1968 SACM became a holding under the name of Société Alsacienne de Participations Industrielle, with its main plant still located in Mulhouse.

## Detail Information for the Pistolet Automatique 7.65mm Modèle 1935A

In 1933 the French military authorities announced an open competition for a new automatic pistol to replace the official revolver model previously in service. One of the principal requirements was for a use of the 7.65 Long Browning cartridge. The test programme extended over a long period, and included a pistol

**Specifications for the French Pistolet Automatique Modèle 1935A**
**System:** Locked breech, recoil operated
**Calibre:** 7.65mm Longue
**Pistol length:** 190mm
**Barrel length:** 106mm
**Grooves:** Four RH twist
**Magazine:** Eight rounds
**Weight (empty):** 741g
**Weight (loaded):** 815g
**Safety:** Thumb lever

designed by Charles Petter in 1934 and patented one year later. Despite fierce competition from pistol designs produced by other well established factories throughout Europe, the Petter weapon was eventually judged to be the most suitable, and was therefore recommended by the French authorities for military use.

The pistol was officially adopted as a regulation army sidearm in that year, and received the identification of Modèle 1935A. It was also submitted for trials by the British War Office in September 1936, but was rejected for military purposes because of its small calibre. Manufacture was undertaken by the SACM factory in Cholet, and continued throughout the following three years, during which time other factories became involved in order to meet the military demand. A modified version of the standard pistol had also been produced by the factory at St Etienne as Model 1935S, which was much simpler in its construction and less complicated for manufacture. It, too, was adopted by the French authorities, in December 1937.

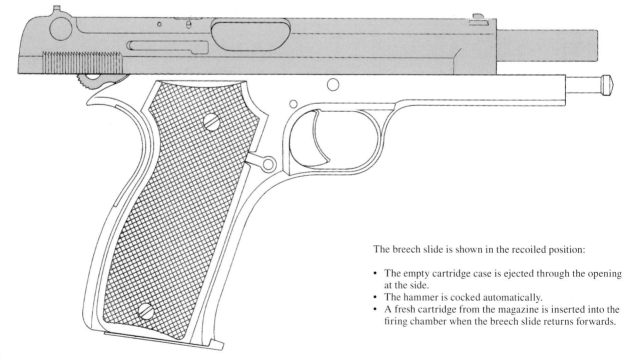

The breech slide is shown in the recoiled position:

- The empty cartridge case is ejected through the opening at the side.
- The hammer is cocked automatically.
- A fresh cartridge from the magazine is inserted into the firing chamber when the breech slide returns forwards.

The outbreak of World War II and the invasion of France by the German army soon resulted in the complete seizure and control of all arms production facilities. As a consequence, the Cholet factory was annexed, and the 1935A pistol was absorbed into the Nazi Foreign Equipment category; it was given the title Pistole 625(f), and throughout the war years it was issued to occupation police and various governing officials in France. After World War II, the Petter design was revised and developed into a 9mm version for the Swiss armed forces.

Although based on the ubiquitous Browning locked breech system, Model 1935A includes a selection of original features in its design. Foremost amongst these were amendments to the breech slide arrangement in order to incorporate a detachable hammer unit at the rear. In the breech locking system, the barrel is held to the breech slide by two ribs and employs two hinged links under the chamber end in a somewhat similar manner to that of the Colt 45. A further development concerned a special mounting of the recoil spring in conjunction with the hinged link assembly. These innovations were all included in the original French patent of March 1935.

**The breech slide:** Contains the extractor, firing pin with spring, a cartridge indicator and the safety lever. The sear, hammer and mainspring assembly is contained in a detachable housing that fits into the back end of the breech slide. The entire unit is inserted into an opening at the rear of the pistol body.

**The recoil spring:** Mounted on its guide tube, this spring extends between a fixed plug at the front and a removable plug at the rear that pivots together with the two links on the breech stop axis.

This enabled the items to be secured in the pistol body as a single assembly.

**The grip plates:** Made of a hardened rubber compound, with each plate secured to the grip by a screw at the top and at the bottom.

**The safety lever:** Located at the rear left side in an upper extension of the breech slide, where it can be rotated to prevent the hammer from reaching the firing pin.

**The magazine:** Retained by an internal catch that can be released by pressing an external button at the left-hand side of the grip. An additional safety feature is included to prevent the weapon from being discharged when the magazine is removed.

## Cartridge Information
Details for the 7.65mm Long cartridge:

**Bullet weight:** 5.8g
**Bullet diameter:** 7.85mm
**Bullet length:** 14.4mm
**Case length:** 19.7mm
**Rim diameter:** 8.5mm
**Cartridge length:** 30.3mm
**Cartridge weight:** 9.3g
**Initial velocity:** 340m/s

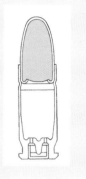

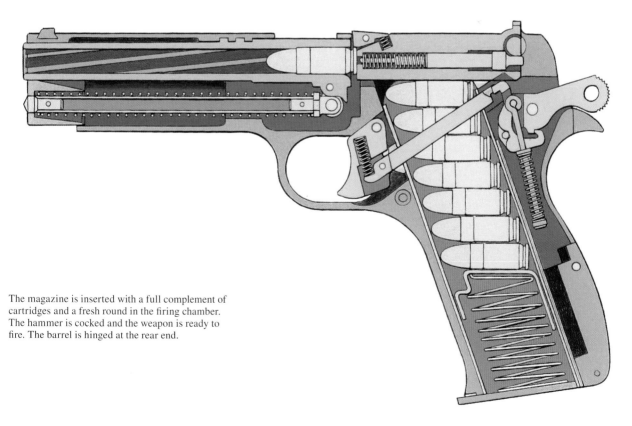

The magazine is inserted with a full complement of cartridges and a fresh round in the firing chamber. The hammer is cocked and the weapon is ready to fire. The barrel is hinged at the rear end.

# 8 Frommer Stop Model 1912 (Hungary)

## 12 Minta Pisztoly (7.65mm Model 1912)

*Regulation sidearm of the Hungarian military forces in both World Wars*

**Factory: Fegyver es Gepgyar, Budapest, Hungary**

In 1886 the Hungarian government had accepted an offer from the German Leowe firm, with credit supplied by the Union Bank of Vienna, to establish a firearms factory in Budapest. However, that venture did not last because of the poor economic situation in Hungary at the time, and the stocks were taken over by Leowe and the Hungarian Bank of Industry and Commerce, who in February 1891 negotiated the formation of the arms and machinery factory as a joint stock company. Predominant among the shareholders was the businessman Izidor Leowe, with finance provided by the bank. Manufacture commenced almost immediately with the production of Mannlicher Model 1889 rifles. The first successful year was 1893, when 65,000 repeating rifles were manufactured for the Austro-Hungarian Ministry of Defence, and this was followed soon afterwards by another order for a further 189,000 weapons. Production then continued to fulfil demands for the

Mannlicher Model 1895, and from the year 1899, the factory was also involved with the production of locks and rear sights for other weapons. As the manufacture of rifles was insufficient to sustain the workforce, other items were sought to augment production, and the firm later acquired the rights to manufacture diesel engines.

From 1901 to 1910 the factory produced a series of self-loading pistols patented by Rudolf Frommer and intended for military use. Examples of these weapons were submitted for testing by the British and United States armies, but were rejected because of their small calibre. It was not until a revised model appeared in 1911 that a design was approved for military use. By the year 1913, an additional factory building had been erected solely for the mass production of the latest pistol design under the leadership of Frommer, who was then a director of the company.

After World War I, the factory continued to maintain its progress by developing several types of sporting arms. International fame was achieved at the Stockholm world championships in 1928, while two years later, a new shotgun was introduced that brought further acclaim to the firm. In 1935 Rudolf Frommer resigned from his position as company director, and the firm was renamed Femaru, Fegyver es Gepgyar RT after an amalgamation with other companies. In the following year, all manufacture of machine tools and diesel engines was terminated, although the output of new pistol designs continued to occupy the plant for many years thereafter, with many thousands produced for the German army.

## Detail Information for the Frommer
## Stop 7.65mm Pisztoly Minta 1912

A Hungarian patent covering the design of this weapon was granted to Rudolf Frommer in September 1911. It was a development of an earlier model manufactured by the armament and machinery plant in 1906, and followed a succession of self-loading

**Specifications for the Frommer**
**Stop 12 Minta Pisztoly**
**System:** Locked breech, recoil operated
**Calibre:** 7.65mm
**Pistol length:** 165mm
**Barrel length:** 98mm
**Grooves:** Six RH twist
**Magazine:** Seven rounds
**Weight (empty):** 580g
**Weight (loaded):** 634g
**Safety:** Grip lever

pistol designs produced from the same factory. The new version was a much more compact version than the previous designs, and was available in both 7.65 and 9mm calibres. It was identified as the 'Frommer Stop', where 'Stop' indicated the unique system by which the bolt was deliberately stopped by a lever on its return to the breech while the barrel continued forwards. It immediately impressed the Hungarian military authorities, who ordered large numbers to equip Honved divisions of the Austro-Hungarian army during World War I. The Hungarian police force was also equipped with this sidearm, while a smaller but otherwise identical version known as 'the Baby' was offered simultaneously to the civilian market as 'the military rifle in the waistcoat pocket'.

In addition to the military firing trials conducted in Hungary, the pistol was also submitted for testing by the British Small Arms Committee in December 1911; however, its relatively low-calibre ammunition failed to satisfy the War Office requirement for a military cartridge size. After World War I, the Stop design was further modified to create a second military version, identified as the Model 1929 and chambered for the 9mm Browning Short cartridge. In 1920 a folding metal butt was proposed for the

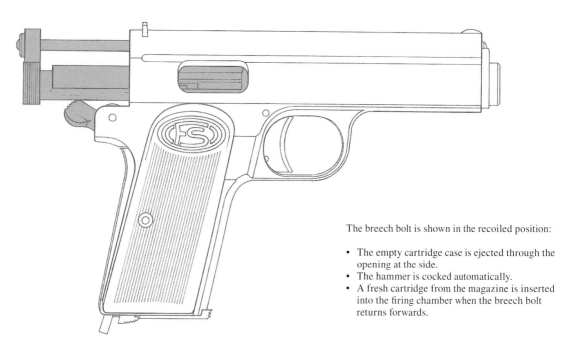

The breech bolt is shown in the recoiled position:

- The empty cartridge case is ejected through the opening at the side.
- The hammer is cocked automatically.
- A fresh cartridge from the magazine is inserted into the firing chamber when the breech bolt returns forwards.

pistol, and it was provided with a folding metal frame attached to the butt, and which extended to form a shoulder piece. Another modification proposed in 1930 was to insert a sleeve within the rifled barrel, which enabled the weapon to fire the .22 Rim Fire cartridge. Manufacture continued until World War II, and is reported to have exceeded 329,000.

This pistol is unusual in having a locked breech system for a comparatively low-powered cartridge, and by the positioning of the recoil springs above the barrel. Its design is a complicated progression from earlier Frommer pistols, using a revised locking arrangement. Locking of the breech is achieved by lugs on a rotating bolt head engaging recesses in the barrel extension. There is no conventional breech slide, as the barrel and breech bolt are both contained within the pistol body. After each discharge, the barrel and breech bolt recoil together and are each returned to the firing position by a separate spring.

**The barrel:** Secured at the front of the pistol body to a collar with a projection that acts on the recoil spring when the pistol is fired, thus causing the bolt to rotate and unlock.

**The recoil spring:** Located in a channel at the top of the pistol body, where it surrounds a breech bolt rod. A separate spring surrounds the back portion of the rod and returns the breech bolt after the recoil spring has first returned the barrel.

**The breech bolt:** Attached at its rear end to a knurled cocking knob that is also connected to a long spring guide rod above. The spring serves to return the bolt to the firing position.

**The magazine:** Held in place by a spring-loaded catch at the bottom rear end of the grip. Cartridges are fed into the firing chamber as the breech bolt returns forwards.

**The firing mechanism:** Consists of an external hammer striking an inertia firing pin located in the breech bolt.

**The safety lever:** Consists of a lever at the back of the grip that pivots at its base to liberate the trigger bar and so allows the weapon to be fired only when the grip is correctly held by hand.

**The grip plates:** Either of wood with a vertical groove pattern and initials FS at the top, or of a hardened rubber compound.

### Cartridge Information
Details for the 7.65mm Frommer cartridge:

**Bullet weight:** 4.8g
**Bullet diameter:** 7.83mm
**Bullet length:** 12.3mm
**Case length:** 17.3mm
**Rim diameter:** 8.4mm
**Cartridge length:** 25mm
**Cartridge weight:** 7.9g
**Initial velocity:** 304m/s

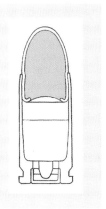

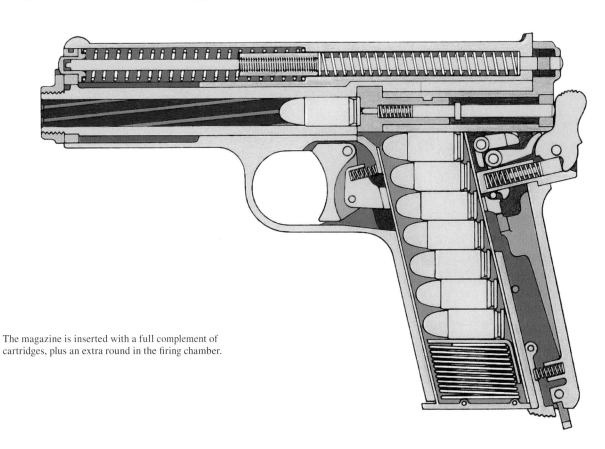

The magazine is inserted with a full complement of cartridges, plus an extra round in the firing chamber.

# 9 Glisenti (Brixia) (Italy)

## Pistola Italiana Modelo 910 (9mm Model 1910)

*Regulation sidearm of the Italian military forces in World War I*

**Factory: Metallurgica Bresciana gia Tempini, Brescia, Italy**

The original concern had been founded as a partnership in 1884 by Giovanni Tempini and two Palotti brothers, who subsequently acquired premises in Brescia for their manufacture of metal goods and cartridge cases. The partnership was dissolved in 1887 and re-established under the company name of Metallurgica Tempini. By 1889 the firm had become a limited company, and continued with the manufacture of metal products for the next fourteen years. Capital investment had been obtained from the Italian Union Bank and certain important German firms. The business was reorganized once more in 1905 to become the Metallurgica Bresciana gia Tempini. By 1907, the increased finances enabled the purchase of the manufacturing plant known as Siderurgica Glisenti, a company that had been actively engaged in producing an extensive range of military weapons since the middle of the nineteenth century. This acquisition included several factories and

iron foundries, plus electrical and engineering works, all located within the Brescia region. Glisenti had also acquired patents for a new self-loading pistol that the factory was about to produce for the Italian Ministry of War, and a contract for an initial quantity of 15,000 pistols had already been received in 1906.

Giovanni Tempini, founder and president of the metalwork enterprise, had retired due to ill health in 1907, at a time when the manufacture of military pistols was becoming an important feature of the company business. A second order for another 15,000 pistols for the Italian military was placed with the Metallurgica during the following year. Throughout the next decade, various other factories belonging to the enterprise at Carcina, Cogosso and Sarezzo were disposed of, and all work was then concentrated at Brescia. In 1920 the firm offered a revised version of the self-loading pistol under the title 'Brixia' as a military weapon, and for the commercial market as a sporting arm. In addition to the pistol, a machinegun capable of a variable rate of fire was patented and developed at the factory in 1930 with a similar title.

The Brescia plant was one of the oldest in the region, and by 1940 its premises had increased from 85,600 square metres to over 128,000. The factory had become well known for its manufacture of both arms and munitions over the years, but at the conclusion of World War II it was incorporated into the expanding Societa Metallurgica Italiana, and underwent radical change in that from then on it manufactured rods and copper tubes.

## Detail Information for the Glisenti (Brixia) Pistola 9mm Modello 1910

The Glisenti model was the first automatic pistol to be officially adopted by the Italian military as a regulation sidearm. It was designed by an Italian army officer named Bethel-Abiel Revelli, who sold the patent for his pistol to the gunmaking firm of Siderurgica Glisenti in 1905. Following the construction and testing of a

**Specifications for the Glisenti (Brixia) Pistola Italiana Modelo 910**
**System:** Semi-locked breech, recoil operated
**Calibre:** 9mm
**Pistol length:** 209mm
**Barrel length:** 95mm
**Grooves:** Six RH twist
**Magazine:** Seven rounds
**Weight (empty):** 870g
**Weight (loaded):** 955g
**Safety:** Grip lever and striker nut

prototype, the design was duly accepted by the Italian army, who placed an initial contract for 15,000 of the new pistol. Unable to fulfil the order, Glisenti sold the manufacturing rights in July 1907 to the Societa Metallurgica, who received a further order for 15,000 pistols in 1908. Despite the change in manufacture the weapon continued to retain its original Glisenti title.

After its adoption by the Italians, the pistol was submitted for trials by the British War Office in November 1907 and again in 1910; it also underwent tests by the United States Ordnance Board in 1912. On each occasion the weapon was rejected because of its calibre, as both authorities required more powerful ammunition for military handguns. Although it is classified as a 9mm pistol, the breech is not positively locked to the barrel but is held by a pivoting block at the moment of discharge, and this system does not permit the use of more powerful 9mm cartridges.

The Glisenti pistol remained in service use by the Italian army for various campaigns throughout World War I, after which it was slightly modified by the Metallurgica factory and offered for sale on the civilian market as the Brixia model. Alterations were

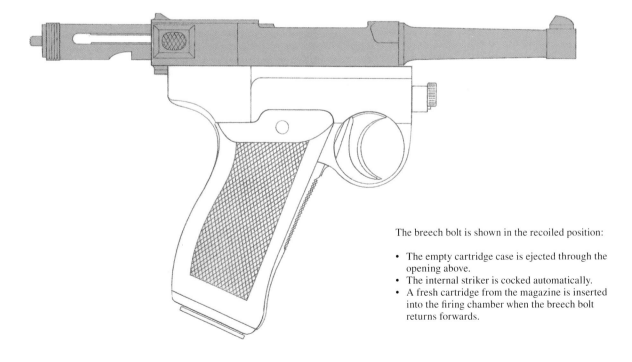

The breech bolt is shown in the recoiled position:

- The empty cartridge case is ejected through the opening above.
- The internal striker is cocked automatically.
- A fresh cartridge from the magazine is inserted into the firing chamber when the breech bolt returns forwards.

made to the general body style, and a version was also produced with an extra-long barrel, adjustable rear sight and shoulder stock attachment. During World War II the pistol continued to be used, although in reduced quantities, as manufacture had ceased entirely. By that time it had been officially replaced by a new 9mm Beretta model as an Italian regulation sidearm.

This weapon is quite complex in construction and operation, but has several interesting features in its design. Instead of having a locked breech, the system operates on a delayed blowback principle, using a rotating locking piece to support the breech recoil. The grip safety feature is unusual in being located at the front of the grip rather than at the rear.

**The barrel:** Screwed into the front of the breech casing to form a complete unit extending the entire length of the pistol. A separate spring, located within the breech casing, returns the barrel forwards after firing. A detachable side plate is fitted to the left side of the pistol and gives access to the firing mechanism and locking piece.

**The breech block:** Square in section and contains the extractor, striker, recoil spring with its guide rod and the safety knob. It fits within the breech casing where it is retained by a transverse wedge. Milled projections at the rear end of the block permit it to be drawn back by hand for cocking the firing mechanism.

**The locking piece:** A pivoted member that engages a notch cut into the lower part of the breech block under pressure from a strong laminar spring.

**The safety device:** Consists of a rotary knob located at the end of the breech block, where it can be turned anticlockwise to lock the striker when the weapon is cocked. Another safety device, consisting of a long lever, is provided at the front of the grip to block the trigger until the weapon is held in the hand.

**The firing mechanism:** Employs a striker, which screws into the recoil spring guide and is contained within the breech block.

**The magazine:** Held in place by a lever pivoted inside the grip, and released by pressure on a semi-circular stud at the base.

**The grip plates:** Of wood with a chequered pattern cut into the surface of the central portion.

## Cartridge Information
Details for the 9mm Glisenti cartridge:

**Bullet weight:** 8g
**Bullet diameter:** 9.02mm
**Bullet length:** 15mm
**Case length:** 19mm
**Rim diameter:** 9.98mm
**Cartridge length:** 29.2mm
**Cartridge weight:** 12.25g
**Initial velocity:** 300m/s

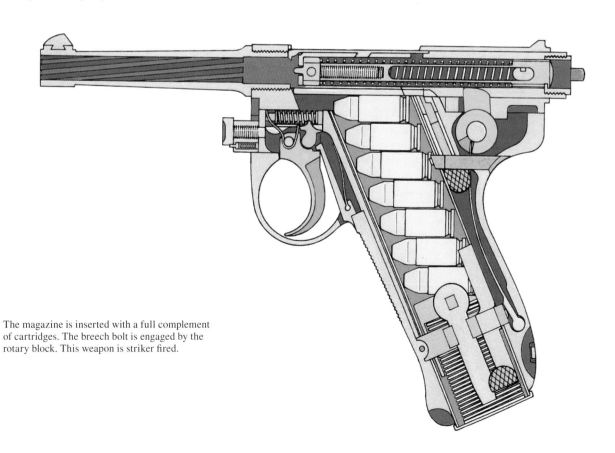

The magazine is inserted with a full complement of cartridges. The breech bolt is engaged by the rotary block. This weapon is striker fired.

# 10  Lahti Model 1935 (Finland)

## *Pistooli L-35 (9mm Model 1935)*

### *Regulation sidearm of the Finnish military forces in World War II*

**Factory: Valtion Kivaaritehdas, Jyvaskyla, Finland**

A factory specifically intended for the manufacture of military small arms was first established by the Finnish government in April 1925, although the official inauguration of new factory buildings took place at Jyvaskyla in southern Finland three years later. The first weapon to be produced at the plant was a light machinegun that had been approved as an official arm for the Finnish army in 1926. This was followed by a self-loading pistol designed for military use by Aimo Lahti, plus various other automatic weapons including a large calibre anti-tank rifle. Sporting guns were also designed and developed at the Jyvaskyla factory during the 1930s. These were principally small-bore rifles manufactured in limited quantities for target shooting by local marksmen. The outbreak of war in October 1939 between Finland and Russia brought about an increased output of war materials at the Jyvaskyla factory, where considerable quantities of automatic small arms were already in mass production to equip the small army of homeland defenders. The high quality of their weapons, which had functioned so well in the arduous conditions of that

conflict, had contributed greatly to a successful outcome for the people of Finland, and increased prosperity to the factory.

Unfortunately, the peace treaty that followed in the spring of 1940 lasted barely a year, and the two countries were once

again engaged in warfare by June 1941, after Finland had joined with Germany in an effort to regain territory yielded to the Soviets earlier. The manufacture of arms and munitions in Finland took precedence over everything else throughout that eventful period. Development continued on further automatic arms, with the design of a new assault rifle being completed at the factory in 1943.

Until 1945, the plant operated under the direct control of the Ministry of Defence, but after the end of World War II it was amalgamated with three other government factories in the same region to become part of the Valtion Metallitehtaat (State Metal Works). Further manufacture of military weapons was suspended at that time, and production became more diversified to include such items as tractors, engines and machinery. Moreover, the firm had become extensively involved with a heavy programme of war reparations that Finland was obliged to pay the Soviet Union as an outcome of World War II. The whole enterprise was eventually incorporated within a joint stock company, Valmet Oy, one of the most prominent engineering firms of Finland.

## Detail Information for the Lahti Pistooli 9mm L-35

A prototype of the Lahti model was initially created in 1929 by Aimo Lahti, who later patented his design in 1932. At that time, he was the chief weapon designer employed by the State Rifle factory in Jyvaskyla, Finland. Serial manufacture of the new pistol was commenced at that factory, with the first five examples being dispatched for acceptance trials by the army. An order for 2,500 pistols was subsequently placed with the factory in January 1936, although deliveries were not possible until the summer of 1938 due to other commitments at the plant. On receipt, each pistol was

**Specifications for the Lahti Model 1935 Pistooli L-35**
**System:** Locked breech, recoil operated
**Calibre:** 9mm Parabellum
**Pistol length:** 239mm
**Barrel length:** 120mm
**Grooves:** Six RH twist
**Magazine:** Eight rounds
**Weight (empty):** 1,250g
**Weight (loaded):** 1,425g
**Safety:** Thumb lever

stamped with an army acceptance mark and weapon identification of L-35. These were first used by the Finnish armed forces during the conflict between Finland and Russia during October 1939 and March 1940.

Production of the Lahti pistol was not particularly rapid, and by the end of November 1940 fewer than 2,000 had been delivered to the military authorities. However, manufacture of the pistol then continued throughout World War II to reach a total of 5,618 by December 1945. Although the L-35 model had been destined primarily for use with the Finnish defence forces, small quantities were also distributed commercially during wartime.

After the war, all manufacture of military weapons was temporarily suspended, and by 1951 the Jyvaskyla factory had been incorporated within a joint stock company as Valmet Oy. Further Lahti pistols were then marketed under the Valmet symbol, with most of these versions being delivered to Sweden

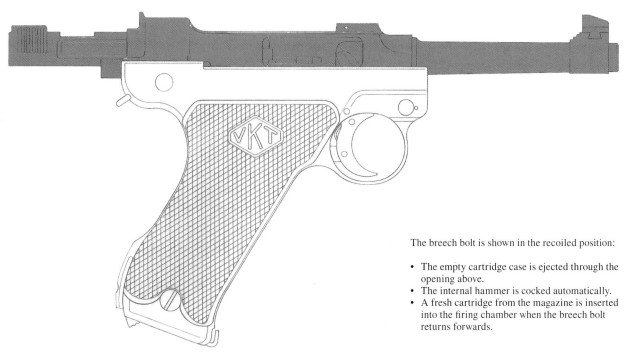

The breech bolt is shown in the recoiled position:

- The empty cartridge case is ejected through the opening above.
- The internal hammer is cocked automatically.
- A fresh cartridge from the magazine is inserted into the firing chamber when the breech bolt returns forwards.

and Israel. Meanwhile, a slightly modified version of the pistol had been manufactured earlier under special licence in Sweden, where it was adopted as the Model 40. Approximately 8,500 pistols were produced in that country during the war for use against Nazi invaders. The fiftieth anniversary of its first introduction was commemorated in 1985 by a special manufacture for collectors.

The Finnish L-35 pistol is a strong, rugged and heavy handgun, whose appearance and handling characteristics reflect the arduous conditions that the weapon was designed to meet. The extremely low temperatures often prevalent in Finland are apt to cause problems with the mechanical operation of the pistol, so an auxiliary breech-opening device is built into the system; it takes the form of a pivoting lever positioned beneath the front of the breech casing, which accelerates the recoil motion of the breech block.

**The barrel:** Screwed into the front of the breech casing to form a complete unit that extends the entire length of the pistol.

**The breech block:** Square in section and contains the extractor, firing pin and spring, together with the recoil spring and its guide rod. Serrations are formed on the rear sides of the block to provide gripping areas for cocking the weapon by hand.

**The locking piece:** Fits like a saddle over the rear portion of the breech block, and engages a recess at the top of the breech casing to lock the system. Angled projections at each side correspond with slots in the pistol body, and these move the locking piece out of engagement as the breech recoils.

**The recoil spring:** Of small diameter, positioned around a long guide rod that passes through a hole at the rear of the pistol body when the weapon is fired.

**The firing system:** Employs an internal hammer and long firing pin positioned at an angle beneath the recoil spring.

**The safety lever:** Located at the left rear side of the grip, and moved back to block the sear in either the cocked or uncocked setting to prevent the weapon from being fired.

**The magazine:** Retained in the grip by a spring-operated catch at the rear of the butt. Some versions are also provided with a slot at the rear face of the grip for the attachment of a shoulder stock.

### Cartridge Information
Details for the 9mm Parabellum cartridge:

**Bullet weight:** 8g
**Bullet diameter:** 9.02mm
**Bullet length:** 15.25mm
**Case length:** 19.3mm
**Rim diameter:** 9.96mm
**Cartridge length:** 29.2mm
**Cartridge weight:** 12.1g
**Initial velocity:** 345m/s

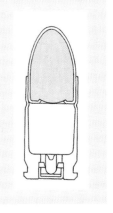

The magazine is inserted with a full complement of cartridges. The breech block is engaged by the vertically rising block.

# 11 Luger Model 1908 (Germany)

## *Pistole Parabellum P08 (9mm Model 1908)*

*Regulation sidearm of the German military forces in both World Wars*

**Factory: Deutsche Waffen und Munitions Fabrik, Berlin, Germany**

The German Arms and Munitions Factory was formed on 10 December 1896 as the result of a merger between prominent German firms engaged in arms production. The new enterprise was under the financial control of Ludwig Loewe & Company in Berlin, which became the centre of administration. Since 1887, the Loewe firm had acquired a controlling interest in the great Mauser works at Oberndorf, and had become one of the first to establish modern mass-production methods in Germany. Following another amalgamation with two gunpowder factories on 14 February 1889, the name Deutsche Metallpatronenfabrik–Karlsruhe was adopted, while other factories at Karlsruhe and Grotzingen were acquired to create the great DWM organization. A new Borchardt automatic pistol was introduced to the commercial market by the Loewe concern in 1893, and production continued for a brief period thereafter. In 1901 the company entered into a patent-sharing agreement with the British armaments firm of Vickers Sons and Maxim, under which the German factory was granted special licence to manufacture and sell certain automatic weapons to certain European countries. Throughout the years

after 1914 the firm became heavily involved with the output of war material.

After World War I, the manufacture of military weapons was reduced considerably by the influence of the Versailles Treaty, and the business became concentrated more towards the private sector. Accordingly, the company trade name was altered in 1922 to Berlin-Karlsruher Industriewerke Aktiengesellschaft. But in May 1930, a vast programme of reorganization was implemented, and all production equipment, together with tools and techni-

cal personnel, was transferred from Berlin to the Mauser plant at Oberndorf. Manufacture was gradually resumed at the new location, and arms production continued there for the expanding armed forces of the future Third Reich.

From the start of World War II in 1939, the output potential of the now huge enterprise was enormous, and vast quantities of all weapons were manufactured throughout the wartime period. The production of automatic pistols was yet another important market feature, and enabled the new plant to secure important military contracts for the supply of pistols. After the end of the war, the business was supervised by a board of trustees; this continued until 1949, when it reverted to the organization Industriewerke Karlsruhe Aktiengesellschaft. Eventually it became known as the Deutsch Industrieanlagen GmbH, and was once again located in Berlin.

## Detail Information for the Luger Pistole 9mm Parabellum Modell 08

The Luger pistol ranks amongst the most famous of all military automatic handguns. It was developed in 1900 by Georg Luger from an original design patented by Hugo Borchardt in 1893 and manufactured by the Berlin firm of Ludwig Leowe. In order to make the weapon more widely acceptable for military purposes, various refinements were introduced and patented by Luger. Following tests conducted in Germany, Switzerland, Britain and the USA, it was first adopted by the Swiss army, who ordered 3,000 of the pistols in 1900. These were in calibre 7.65mm, while a later version in 9mm calibre was subsequently accepted by the

## Specifications for the Luger Model 1908 Pistole Parabellum P08

**System:** Locked breech, recoil operated
**Calibre:** 9mm Parabellum
**Pistol length:** 220mm
**Barrel length:** 102mm
**Grooves:** Six RH twist
**Magazine:** Eight rounds
**Weight (empty):** 850g
**Weight (loaded):** 939g
**Safety:** Thumb lever

Imperial German Marine in 1904. By that time, its manufacture had been undertaken by the German Arms and Munitions Factory in Berlin.

The unusual design of the new pistol had aroused considerable interest abroad, and resulted in its adoption for military use by several other nations throughout the world. Approximately 8,000 had been produced for the German navy, although a much larger order was placed by the imperial army in 1908. By the year 1911, a total of 160,000 pistols had been supplied to various countries, the vast majority being those delivered to the armed forces of Germany. Luger pistols had been given an additional title of Parabellum, meaning 'for war', and were consequently used in great numbers during World War I. As demand for the pistol increased, other factories began to participate in its manu-

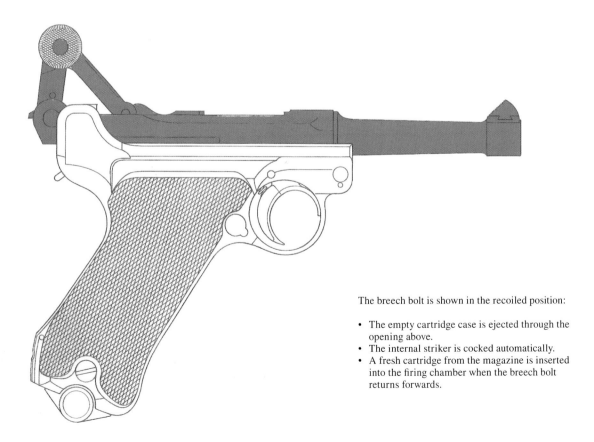

The breech bolt is shown in the recoiled position:

- The empty cartridge case is ejected through the opening above.
- The internal striker is cocked automatically.
- A fresh cartridge from the magazine is inserted into the firing chamber when the breech bolt returns forwards.

facture, which continued until the armistice of 1918. After the war, further manufacture in Germany was forbidden, but production was eventually resumed in 1924 by the Swiss, and by the Mauser factory after 1930. All military production ceased in 1942 after some 300,000 pistols had been produced by Mauser, and the Parabellum model remained in service during World War II until it was finally replaced by the Walther P38.

The hinged breech arrangement of the Luger model is unique in pistol design, although it had appeared much earlier on the Maxim machinegun. Locking of the breech on discharge is achieved by the bracing of two hinged levers, which are liberated against curved ramps at the rear of the pistol body when the weapon is fired. This causes the central hinge to rise as the entire upper unit recoils and draws the breech block away from the barrel.

**The barrel:** Screwed into an extension provided with two arms that embrace the breech block and hinge-joint links. A locking bolt at the front left side secures the extension to the pistol body.

**The breech block:** Contains the extractor, the striker with its spring and the guide retainer. One end of the extractor is raised into view to indicate when a cartridge is in the firing chamber. The block is joined to a front link arm hinged to a rear link that pivots at the back of the barrel extension. Large circular knobs projecting from each side of the rear link aid in drawing back the block by hand.

**The recoil spring:** Lies within the grip behind the back of the magazine. Its guide rod is connected to the rear link by a bell-crank lever and coupling link.

**The firing mechanism:** Employs a striker that is cocked against its spring guide. A detachable cover plate located at the front left-hand side of the pistol body gives access to the trigger mechanism.

**The magazine:** Held in position within the grip by a catch at the upper front edge. The magazine base is either of wood, plastic or metal, and has a circular button at each side to assist removal.

**The safety lever:** Located at the upper rear left side of the pistol body, and operated to prevent the cocked striker from being released.

**The grip plates:** Normally of wood with a chequered pattern cut into the exterior surface. The top of each plate fits into the pistol body and is retained by a single screw at the base.

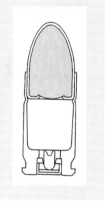

**Cartridge Information**
Details for the 9mm Parabellum cartridge:

**Bullet weight:** 8g
**Bullet diameter:** 9.02mm
**Bullet length:** 15.1mm
**Case length:** 19mm
**Rim diameter:** 10mm
**Cartridge length:** 28.85mm
**Cartridge weight:** 12.1g
**Initial velocity:** 345m/s

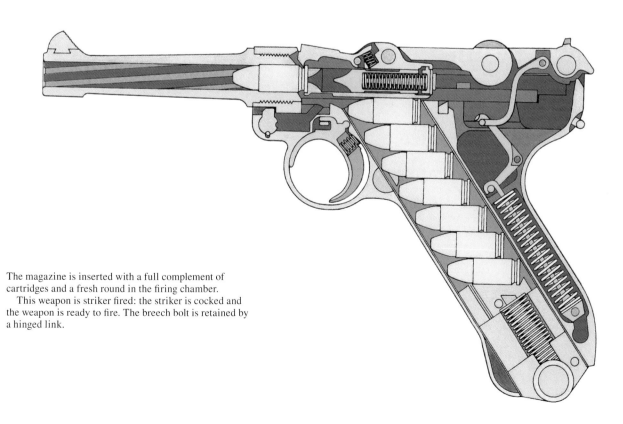

The magazine is inserted with a full complement of cartridges and a fresh round in the firing chamber.
This weapon is striker fired: the striker is cocked and the weapon is ready to fire. The breech bolt is retained by a hinged link.

# 12 Mauser Model 1896 (Germany)

## *Feederlepistole C96 (7.63mm Model 1896)*

*Regulation sidearm of the German military forces in World War I*

**Factory: Waffenfabrik Mauser,
Oberndorf am Neckar, Germany**

The Mauser arms factory was initially founded in 1872 as a small partnership of the two brothers, Paul and Wilhelm Mauser. A financial investment of 800,000 marks from the Württembergische Vereinsbank of Stuttgart enabled Gebrüder Mauser to become a limited company two years later, when the government arsenal at Oberndorf was purchased to fulfil an order for 100,000 Mauser system rifles for the German army. At the successful conclusion of that contract in 1876, production was maintained by a request from China for 26,000 rifles, followed by a consignment of 100,000 produced for the government of Serbia in 1881.

Wilhelm Mauser died in 1882, leaving control of the business to his brother Paul. Financial directorship was eventually taken over by the Württemberg Federal Bank, allowing the business to operate as a joint stock company from April 1884. In that same year, Mauser introduced the first German repeater rifle, a weapon that was also manufactured in huge numbers. The business structure changed again in 1888 when the Berlin firm of Ludwig Loewe & Company acquired a controlling interest. This also led to an enlargement of the Oberndorf plant and the installation of new machinery to cope with large arms contracts from the German government.

After the creation of a Mauser five-round clip loading system in 1888, more rifles were ordered by Turkey, Argentina and Spain during the next few years. By 1896, the firm had become one of the pioneers in the field of self-loading pistols by manufacturing the first truly successful weapon of that type. One year later, the newly formed Deutsches Waffen und Munitionsfabriken acquired the remaining stock from Mauser and took over complete control of future business, the company then becoming known as Waffenfabrik Mauser Aktiengesellschaft. In April 1898, the latest version of the Mauser system rifle was officially adopted for use by the German army, with nearly 300,000 being built at the Oberndorf factory by 1907.

During the turn of the century a considerable amount of design work was undertaken at Oberndorf involving both pistols and rifles in an effort to achieve successful automatic military weapons. From 1907 until 1912 no fewer than sixteen patents were registered in Germany for developments in self-loading pistols alone. 1910 witnessed the introduction of an unlocked breech pistol, and improved versions were manufactured to a total of one million. When Paul Mauser died in 1914, the factory was totally committed to arms production throughout both World Wars.

## Detail Information for the Mauser 7.63mm Feederlepistole C96

Despite being patented and manufactured under the name of Mauser, this weapon was actually designed in 1894 by the brothers Friedrich and Fidel Feederle, who were employed at the Oberndorf factory. It was initially constructed in several versions and in different calibres. Eventually, a special 7.63mm high velocity cartridge was developed for use with the pistol.

## Specifications for the Mauser Model 1896 Feederlepistole C96

**System:** Locked breech, recoil operated
**Calibre:** 7.63mm Mauser
**Pistol length:** 252mm
**Barrel length:** 98mm
**Grooves:** Six RH twist
**Magazine:** Ten rounds
**Weight (empty):** 1,170g
**Weight (loaded):** 1,277g
**Safety:** Thumb lever

A number of minor modifications were introduced to the design after the first few years of manufacture, by which time 35,000 pistols had been produced. Some of these weapons had previously been supplied to the Italian navy, although they were not adopted by any other nation to serve as an official sidearm. Nevertheless, the Mauser model did achieve considerable success commercially throughout the world, and many were acquired by private individuals. As a potential military sidearm it was expensive to manufacture, and was normally used as a substitute weapon rather than an official regulation pistol. It certainly saw extensive use by the German army throughout the World War I, and in order to standardize ammunition, the Mauser factory was requested by the Weapons Testing Commission for the pistol to be converted to accept the regulation 9mm ammunition. A total of 150,000 were then made by Mauser in that calibre, and supplied to troops during the war in addition to their standard-issue pistols.

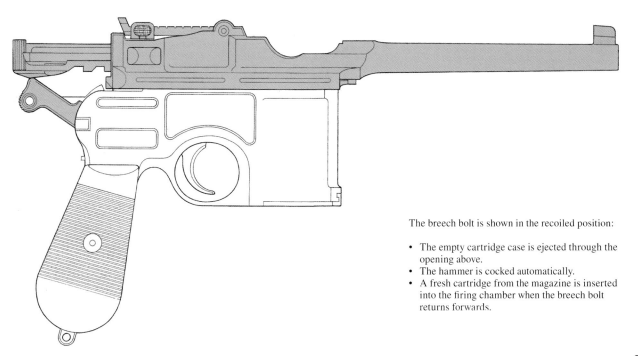

The breech bolt is shown in the recoiled position:

- The empty cartridge case is ejected through the opening above.
- The hammer is cocked automatically.
- A fresh cartridge from the magazine is inserted into the firing chamber when the breech bolt returns forwards.

After the Armistice in 1918, the Treaty of Versailles prohibited further manufacture of military weapons, with the result that all existing supplies were then consigned to store. Production was resumed again in 1922 and continued until 1939. During that period approximately 660,000 had been produced, and many were reissued to units for further use by Germany in World War II. Throughout forty years of its production very few changes had been made to the original nineteenth-century design.

The Mauser pistol, for all its outdated appearance, was a much revered and effective military handgun. It had a reputation for accuracy, and fired a cartridge of high velocity. Although it is quite complicated in construction, the component parts in its mechanism are connected without the use of screws. Locking of the barrel to the breech is achieved by projections on a rising block engaging recesses under the breech bolt. The block is lowered out of engagement as the breech recoils on firing. In an alternative form, the pistol was converted into a cavalry carbine and adapted for fully automatic fire. Known as the Schnellfeuerpistole, it also differed from the standard model in being loaded from below by a detachable magazine.

**The breech bolt:** Square in section and contains the extractor, the recoil spring, and the long firing pin and its spring. Side projections at the rear are provided as an aid in cocking the weapon by hand. Two slots are cut into the under surface to receive the locking block.

**The locking block:** Has two projections on its upper surface to engage with the breech bolt, and an extension at the lower rear end that moves the block out of engagement when the weapon is fired.

**The barrel:** Incorporated into a rectangular extension, which also contains an adjustable rear sight mounted on its upper surface. The sight is calibrated in 50-metre increments to a maximum of 1,000 metres.

**The magazine:** Unusual in being located ahead of the trigger guard; cartridges are fed into the top of it from stripper clips.

**The safety lever:** Positioned within the rear of the pistol body at the left side of the hammer. When the lever is in a vertical position the hammer is withdrawn from the firing pin.

**The grip plates:** Normally wooden, with central areas cut in a pattern of horizontal serrations. Both plates are secured in place by a single bolt on one plate entering a nut on the opposite plate.

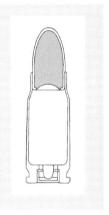

**Cartridge Information**
Details for the 7.63mm Mauser cartridge +:

**Bullet weight:** 5.5g
**Bullet diameter:** 7.83mm
**Bullet length:** 13.6mm
**Case length:** 25.1mm
**Rim diameter:** 9.95mm
**Cartridge length:** 34.40mm
**Cartridge weight:** 10.7g
**Initial velocity:** 443m/s

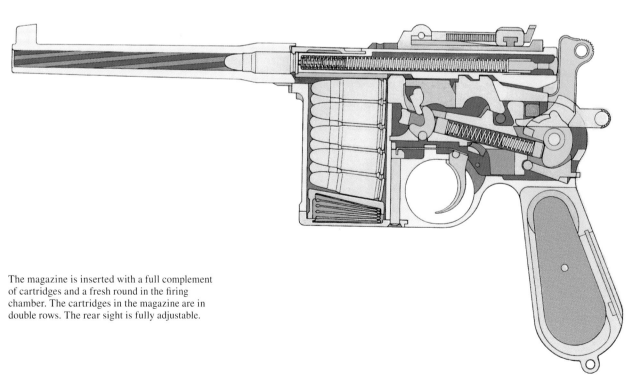

The magazine is inserted with a full complement of cartridges and a fresh round in the firing chamber. The cartridges in the magazine are in double rows. The rear sight is fully adjustable.

# 13 Nambu Model 1925 (Japan)

## *Nambu Type 14 Year (8mm Model 1925)*

### *Regulation sidearm of the Japanese military forces in both World Wars*

**Factory: Nagoya Arsenal, Nagoya, Japan**

The history of Nagoya Arsenal began in the year 1904 when the Atsuta Ordnance Factory (Atsuta Heiki Seizosho) was purchased by the imperial Japanese army and placed under the direction of the Tokyo Arsenal. Originally known as the Tetsudo Shanyo Seizosho, the company had been engaged in the manufacture of rolling stock, but under the new administration, their output was adapted to the production of ammunition trucks and steel boats. During World War I, this factory produced aircraft engines and fuselages for the expanding air power of Japan.

The manufacture of engines was then taken over from Atsuta in 1918 by the Chigusa Machinery factory; one year later, both those factories were placed under the supervision of a newly formed military arsenal (Rikugun Zoheisho Nagoya Kosho) at Nagoya, the capital city of Aichi Prefecture in central Honshu. This was at a time when Japanese industry was continuing to develop under the dominant influence of the military. When Emperor Yoshihito died in December 1926 and the country had proclaimed a new era of Showa, there was a sudden revival of the old Japanese imperial ideology. Hundreds of young men were

being trained as qualified engineers at both Chigusa and Atsuta plants.

Other factories and machine shops within the Nagoya vicinity were later annexed to create a central production source with

its headquarters operating from the Atsuta Ordnance factory. Those additions included the arms factories of Takakura in 1937, Toriimatsu in 1939, Takagi in 1941, Yanaizu in 1944 and Suruga in 1945. As each factory was added to the military arsenal the word 'arms' was dropped from its title. Of the total output from Japan's eight arsenals during the twenty years from 1926, Nagoya was responsible for 11 per cent of production, using 18 per cent of the total workforce.

Between 1927 and 1932, the factories of Nagoya Arsenal manufactured 8,000 Type 14 pistols for the imperial Japanese forces, while development of another automatic pistol in 1934 provided even more work for the factory. The imperial Japanese army and navy had become dominant powers in Japanese politics throughout that period, by which time a brief conflict between Japan and China in 1937 also served to increase the manufacture of weapons. Nagoya Arsenal was then employing some 43,000 workers. In addition to the earlier production of automatic pistols, a further 232,000 handguns of all types were constructed for Japanese forces during World War II.

## Detail Information for the Nambu 8mm Kenju Juyonen Shiki

This pistol bears the name of its designer, Kijiro Nambu, an officer serving with the imperial Japanese army. It was a development of another handgun created by Nambu in 1904, and became the first automatic pistol to be adopted for use by the Japanese military. Identified as Type 14, it represents the year 1925, or fourteenth year of the Emperor Taisho reign in Japan. The weapon was issued to troops in a leather holster of generous capacity, which also contained an extra magazine, cleaning rod and firing pin. An 8mm bottle-necked cartridge had been developed specially

## Specifications for the Nambu Model 1925 Nambu Type 14 Year

**System:** Locked breech, recoil operated
**Calibre:** 8mm Nambu
**Pistol length:** 230mm
**Barrel length:** 116mm
**Grooves:** Six RH twist
**Magazine:** Eight rounds
**Weight (empty):** 850g
**Weight (loaded):** 909g
**Safety:** Thumb lever

for use with the Nambu pistol, and required a locked breech system consisting of a pivoting block engaging the underside of the breech bolt.

For the first fifteen years of manufacture the design remained virtually unaltered, but by 1940, various improvements had been made to facilitate its operation during winter conditions. This had resulted from the experience gained from earlier campaigns in northern China and Manchuria during the Sino-Japanese War of 1937, when the Type 14 model had been used extensively by Japanese officers and NCOs. The most noticeable alteration was an enlargement of the trigger guard in order to accept the finger of a heavily gloved hand during winter conditions. Total manufacture of that particular version has been estimated to be nearly 20,000.

The Nambu pistol continued in production for the military and was later used during the western Pacific island battles of World War II. It is recorded that well over 320,000 pistols were produced during the twenty-year period of its manufacture.

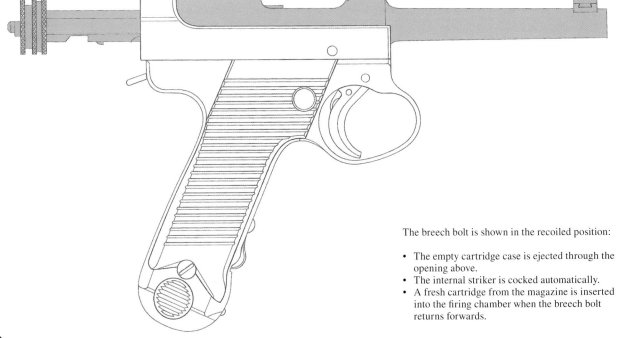

The breech bolt is shown in the recoiled position:

- The empty cartridge case is ejected through the opening above.
- The internal striker is cocked automatically.
- A fresh cartridge from the magazine is inserted into the firing chamber when the breech bolt returns forwards.

Several Japanese arsenals were involved with the production, and various factory symbols were applied to the pistol in its identification, together with dates concerning its manufacture. Those arsenals also included a factory operating under the name of Nambu Seizosho.

The external appearance and general characteristic of this weapon is typically Japanese in styling. The acute angle of grip presents a comfortable feel in handling the pistol. An unusual feature of the construction is a detachable trigger guard assembly, which can be removed from the pistol, together with the trigger sub-assembly, by pulling it down through sloping grooves in front of the grip.

**The barrel:** Formed together with a tubular extension at the rear, which runs almost the entire length of the pistol.

**The breech bolt:** Fitted within the barrel extension and contains the extractor, the striker with its spring and spring guide, plus two recoil springs; the whole assembly is held to the pistol body by a large circular nut at the rear. The breech is held to the barrel during firing by a spring-operated locking block.

**The locking block:** Positioned beneath the barrel extension; it has an upper projection that enters a recess beneath the breech bolt to retain it in position. When the weapon is fired, the locking block is rotated out of engagement to release the breech.

**The recoil springs:** Of small diameter, and lie within semi-circular grooves along both sides of the breech bolt.

**The safety lever:** Positioned at the left side of the pistol body directly above the trigger guard. Turning the lever to the rear rotates an inner stem to block the trigger bar and prevent firing.

**The magazine:** Can be rapidly loaded by pulling down the cartridge platform until it is held in the lowest position while fresh rounds are inserted more conveniently from above.

**The grip plates:** Normally of wood, and cut with a pattern of horizontal grooves. Each plate is retained by a single screw at the base, and bored to receive the magazine release catch.

**The lanyard loop:** Fitted to the rear of the pistol body below the circular breech nut to receive a cord lanyard.

**Cartridge Information**
Details for the 8mm Nambu cartridge:

Bullet weight: 6.4g
Bullet diameter: 8.13mm
Bullet length: 15.2mm
Case length: 21.4mm
Rim diameter: 10.5mm
Cartridge length: 31.7mm
Cartridge weight: 11.5g
Initial velocity: 325m/s

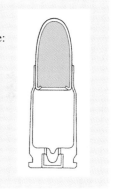

The magazine is inserted with a full complement of cartridges. This weapon is striker fired. The breech bolt is engaged by a spring-operated lever.

# 14  Radom Model 1935 (Poland)

## *Pistolet VIS Wzor 35 (9mm Model 1935)*

### *Regulation sidearm of the Polish military forces in World War II*

**Factory: Fabryka Broni w Radomiu, Radom, Poland**

The State factory of small arms was established as a government-owned enterprise on a decision by the Ministry of Military Affairs to develop and expand a modern Polish arms industry. Since the end of World War I, Polish forces had been mainly equipped with arms from abroad – an arrangement that was not totally desirable when considering the unhappy geographical situation of Poland. In the immediate post-war period, the 600,000-strong Polish army was still occupied in protecting the boundaries between countries in the east and in the west, and it was considered vital that an independent supply of weapons should be established with a minimum of delay. Work began on the erection of new factory buildings in the spring of 1923 at a large open site approximately 60 miles (102km) south of Warsaw near the outskirts of Radom, a town with a thriving industrial centre. Being so close to an important railway junction and having all the transportation facilities necessary, it proved to be an excellent choice for the new factory, and possessed ample scope for any future expansion. Production during the first three years of operation concentrated mainly on Mauser rifles built under special licence agreements with the German firm.

By 1928, annual production had exceeded 40,000 weapons, and this rose to 54,600 in the following year. An arrangement with the Nagant company in Liège, Belgium, also enabled the factory to manufacture the Nagant gas-seal revolvers throughout the early 1930s for the Polish cavalry divisions, until that model was finally displaced by an automatic pistol as an official military sidearm. For the commercial market, there was simultaneous production of a Model 31 sports rifle; however, during the period of the world financial trade recession that followed, a large proportion of the factory activities were absorbed by repairs to earlier patterns of the Model 98 service rifle. When the VIS automatic pistol was introduced, the plant re-tooled for mass production of the new weapon in 1936. Unfortunately, due to events that transpired, the manufacture of all weapons at the factory was then brought to an abrupt halt: when the German armed forces captured the Radom plant on 11 September 1939, administrative control was transferred to the Steyr-Daimler-Puch firm in Austria, where arms production was maintained for the Nazi war effort. All existing supplies of Polish weapons were thereafter appropriated by the Waffenamt for distribution to the occupation forces.

## Detail Information for the Radom
## 9mm Pistolet VIS Wzor 35

While the Radom pistol bears a considerable likeness to the American Colt model, there are some internal modifications to justify its originality. The principal difference lies in the method of unlocking the barrel from the breech during the recoil action, which is achieved by incorporating a cam as part of the barrel itself rather than a link. In addition to a unique safety arrange-

**Specifications for the Radom Model
1935 Pistolet VIS Wzor 35**
**System:** Locked breech, recoil operated
**Calibre:** 9mm Parabellum
**Pistol Length:** 211mm
**Barrel Length:** 114mm
**Grooves:** Six RH twist
**Magazine:** Eight rounds
**Weight (empty):** 1,020g
**Weight (loaded):** 1,106g
**Safety:** Grip lever

ment, an improvement to the design of the recoil spring assembly allowed it to be withdrawn from the pistol body as a complete unit. The design was duly patented in Poland by Piotr Wilniewczyc in February 1932, and officially adopted into service by the Polish military in 1936 to replace the existing revolver. During the firing trials, it was suggested that if the Radom pistol were to be issued to cavalry regiments there would be a problem of the hammer remaining cocked after each firing, with the undesirable prospect of holstering the pistol in that condition. As a consequence, Wilniewczyc decided to introduce a special device to lower the hammer.

The initial production figure amounted to 3,000 pistols, and these were of alloy steel rather than carbon steel, while all featured a long groove cut into the rear of the grip for a shoulder stock attachment. There was no provision of these weapons for the commercial market since the entire production was intended

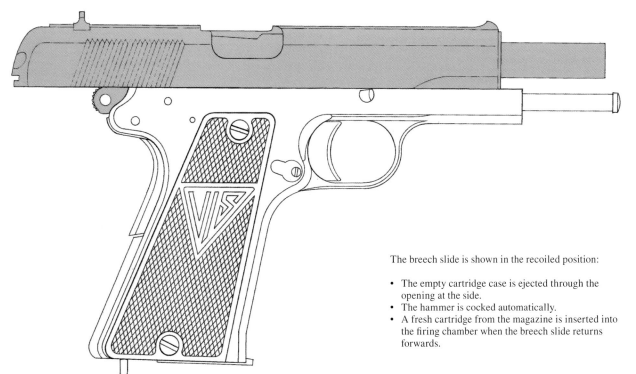

The breech slide is shown in the recoiled position:

- The empty cartridge case is ejected through the opening at the side.
- The hammer is cocked automatically.
- A fresh cartridge from the magazine is inserted into the firing chamber when the breech slide returns forwards.

solely for the Polish military. Before the German invasion of September 1939, more than 49,000 had been manufactured. The entire stock of Radom pistols was then appropriated by the occupation forces, who controlled all further production for the Nazi war effort. Listed under the category of captured foreign arms, the pistol received a new title of Pistole 35(p), and was issued to various police units. Some manufacture was also undertaken by the Steyr factory in Austria. A total in excess of 300,000 Radom pistols had been produced by the end of World War II.

The title 'VIS' applied to this weapon is a Latin word for 'power', since its rugged construction allows it to shoot high-powered 9mm cartridges with safety. Being intended as a cavalry weapon designed for single-handed operation while the rider maintained control of his mount, the Radom pistol was given a special safety feature: when the hammer remained in a cocked position, it could be safely lowered by operation of a lever, which also moved the firing pin to prevent discharge. Other levers are to secure the breech slide in position when the weapon is being disassembled, or when the last round has been fired from the magazine.

**The breech slide:** Contains the extractor, and the firing pin with its spring and retainer plate. Internal grooves are machined from its inner surface to receive an engagement with the barrel. A special lever to lower the hammer is fitted at the left rear side.

**The recoil spring:** The spring and its guide tube make up part of an assembly with an auxiliary spring and end stops. It lies in a small housing at the front end of the breech slide. The whole assembly can be removed from the pistol as a complete unit.

**The barrel:** Provided with locking ribs on its upper surface, and is machined with a solid lug extending from below the chamber.

**The magazine:** Contained within the grip and can be released by operation of a button at the forward left side of the grip.

**Safety lever:** Fitted at the rear of the grip to prevent the pistol from being fired until it is held correctly for shooting.

**The grip plates:** Normally of black moulded synthetic material with a chequered pattern and a symbol on each plate: the initials 'FB' represent the factory (Fabryka Broni), while VIS is the pistol title. The plates are held to the grip by a screw at the top and another at the bottom. The broad angle towards the base of the grip also enables the weapon to fit comfortably in the hand.

### Cartridge Information

Details of the 9mm Parabellum cartridge:

**Bullet weight:** 8g
**Bullet diameter:** 9.02mm
**Bullet length:** 15.25mm
**Case length:** 19.3mm
**Rim diameter:** 9.96mm
**Cartridge length:** 29.2mm
**Cartridge weight:** 12.1g
**Initial velocity:** 345m/s

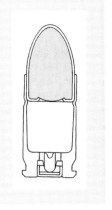

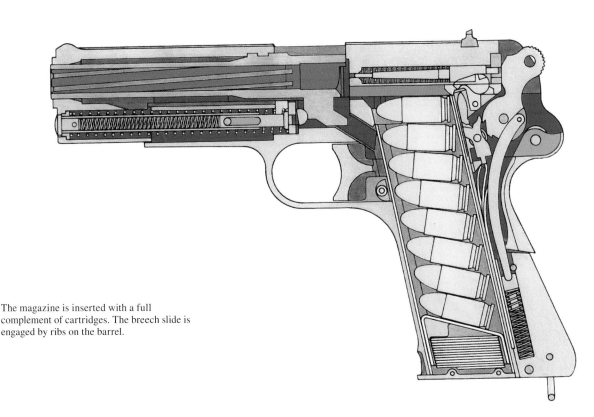

The magazine is inserted with a full complement of cartridges. The breech slide is engaged by ribs on the barrel.

# 15 Roth Model 1907 (Austro-Hungary)

## *Repetierpistole M7 (8mm Model 1907)*

**Regulation sidearm of the Austro-Hungarian military forces in World War I**

**Factory: G. Roth Aktiengesellschaft, Vienna, Austria**

Since the year 1867, the Roth family business had been involved with the large-scale production of ammunition material, to become the most important manufacturer in Austria. The acquisition of other factories enabled the firm to expand considerably, with iron foundries and steel plants in Vienna producing all types of metalware, including cartridge cases and engineering material. When a new factory was constructed at Pressburg in Bratislavia, followed by a powder mill established in Lichtenworth, it enabled the firm to undertake further research on explosives and to concentrate more on the manufacture of that material and modern ammunition for the Austro-Hungarian military. It was this focus that led the factory to venture into the development of new weapons.

After the year 1895, experiments were conducted and patents registered for new types of automatic firearms devised by Wasa Theodorovic and Karel Krnka, both of whom were then engineers

associated with the Vienna plant. Patents mainly concerned handguns, and while the Roth firm did not have the facilities for the mass production of such weapons, permission was given to the Austrian arms factory in Steyr and the Hungarian arms factory in Budapest for licensed manufacture to commence.

Meanwhile the Roth factory continued to be involved with the manufacture of ammunition for various weapons, as well as special loading devices for automatic pistols. In 1905 the business was officially registered as 'G. Roth Metallwaren & Munitionfabriken', but by 1908 it became known as Georg Roth Aktiengesellschaft, with factories established at Felizdorf, Steinabruckl and Malzendorf, in addition to those in Vienna and Lichtenworth. They were involved with the production and sale of all types of explosive, as well as ammunition material, arms, armour, metalware, machines and vehicles of all kinds.

Another Roth facility in Pozsony operated separately from the company and was converted into an independent factory in 1918. The business was still functioning as a family concern in 1921, with Emil Roth as president of the company and his brother Karl Roth as vice president. Three years later, the Roth company still controlled no fewer than six plants, including an iron foundry, machinery factory, machine and tool factory, engine plant, metal works and ammunition factory. Despite embracing such a large source of manufacture, the company did not generate sufficient business to remain sustainable, and it was finally liquidated in 1927 with assets of S1,000,000.

## Detail Information for the Roth 8mm Repetierpistole M7

As one of the earliest locked breech pistols, the Roth model had been designed specifically for use as a cavalry sidearm, and was officially adopted by the Austrian Military Technical Commis-

## Specifications for the Roth Model 1907 Repetierpistole M7

**System:** Locked breech, recoil operated
**Calibre:** 8mm
**Pistol length:** 243mm
**Barrel length:** 128mm
**Grooves:** Four RH twist
**Magazine:** Ten rounds
**Weight (empty):** 1,000g
**Weight (loaded):** 1,106g
**Safety:** None

sion in December 1907. It fires special 8mm cartridges that are loaded from a ten-round charger inserted above the open breech. The firing mechanism differs from other automatic pistols, and the striker does not remain cocked on recoil of the breech: it is cocked and released solely by trigger action. The design evolved as a development of earlier Roth handguns that had been based on a rotary breech bolt concept patented by Wasa Theodorovic and further improved by Karel Krnka.

While the Roth factory was not directly involved with its manufacture, several attempts were made by the company to arouse military interest in the pistol from other nations. In May 1909 a version of the Roth pistol in 11mm calibre was submitted for testing by the British Small Arms Committee, although it was not adopted for military purposes. A similar model was also tested by the American authorities at Springfield Armory in 1911, with the same result. Manufacture of the 8mm Roth model for the Austro-Hungarian army actually took place at the Steyr factory in Austria, and later at the Hungarian Fegyvergyar plant in Buda-

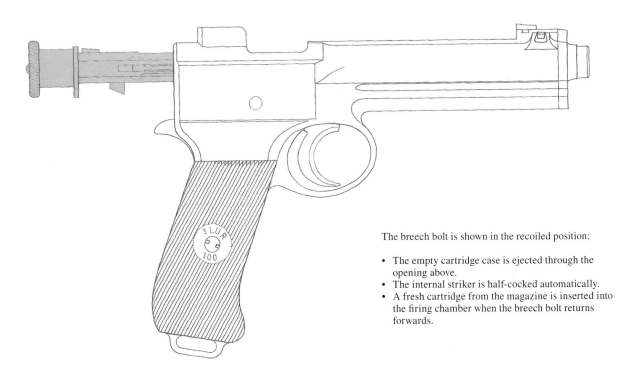

The breech bolt is shown in the recoiled position:

- The empty cartridge case is ejected through the opening above.
- The internal striker is half-cocked automatically.
- A fresh cartridge from the magazine is inserted into the firing chamber when the breech bolt returns forwards.

pest. Production at Steyr reached its height prior to 1914, when approximately 55,000 were manufactured, before the weapon was succeeded by the more powerful 9mm Steyr M12 and production was then diverted to that model.

In Hungary, manufacture continued during World War I with a further 35,000 pistols, all of which were supplied to units of Honved regiments. Despite being considered unnecessary, some examples were actually constructed with a manual safety device to block movement of the cocking piece, while others are known to have been fitted with a detachable shoulder stock.

The construction and operation of this weapon is unusual. In its intended role as a military sidearm, it is complicated in design and therefore expensive to manufacture. Nevertheless, at the time of its manufacture the pistol fulfilled its purpose in equipping the armies of Austria and Hungary with an effective self-loading handgun. It is a large and heavy weapon, but well suited as a cavalry pistol in having a straightforward firing system and a large-capacity magazine. The breech locking arrangement involves studs on the barrel engaging with a helical slot in the breech sleeve. Unlocking of the breech is achieved by a rotary action of the barrel during its recoil motion, which also sets the striker at a half-cocked position. Firing could then only be achieved by a deliberate pull on the trigger, in which respect it differed from other self-loading pistols of the period.

**The breech sleeve:** Extends the entire length of the pistol and contains the extractor, plus a striker and its spring, the latter items being secured by a circular nut at the rear end.

**The barrel:** Contained within a tubular sleeve, and provided with guide studs at the muzzle end and locking studs at the centre. It is held in place by engagement with a circular cap at the front of the pistol body, and locked into a helical slot in the breech sleeve.

**The recoil spring:** Occupies a position beneath the barrel, and has a short guide stud at the rear end to act directly on the trigger.

**Safety device:** Not fitted to the pistol: it was considered superfluous due to the unique cocking arrangement, in which the weapon would only discharge by action of the trigger.

**The magazine:** Held within the grip and contains ten cartridges that are loaded by a charger from above the breech.

**The grip plates:** Of wood, cut with a chequered pattern, and each secured in place by a single screw at the centre.

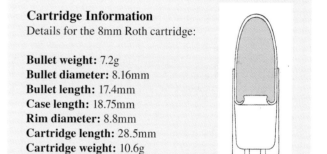

**Cartridge Information**
Details for the 8mm Roth cartridge:

**Bullet weight:** 7.2g
**Bullet diameter:** 8.16mm
**Bullet length:** 17.4mm
**Case length:** 18.75mm
**Rim diameter:** 8.8mm
**Cartridge length:** 28.5mm
**Cartridge weight:** 10.6g
**Initial velocity:** 365m/s

The magazine is inserted with a full complement of cartridges and a fresh round in the firing chamber. This weapon is striker fired. The striker is cocked and the weapon is ready to fire.

# 16 Steyr Model 1912 (Austria)

## *Repetierpistole M12 (9mm Model 1912)*

**Regulation sidearm of the Austrian military forces in World War I**

**Factory: Osterreichische Waffenfabriks Gesellschaft, Steyr, Upper Austria**

An arms factory at Steyr in Upper Austria was first established as a joint stock company on 1 August 1869 under the directorship of the renowned gunsmith Joseph Werndl, who had incorporated several other local arms workshops to form the new enterprise. A special licence was granted in 1873 for the manufacture of 500,000 Mauser rifles to fulfil a contract from the Prussian War Ministry, and this kept the factory occupied for the next two years. Further large orders from various nations throughout the world continued during the 1880s, when, with a workforce that had almost doubled in size, the output of weapons from the Steyr factory surpassed all other prominent arms makers.

In 1882, a limited number of self-loading pistols based on an invention of Anton Schonberger were constructed, and became one of the very first handguns of that type to be manufactured commercially. After the turn of the century the factory produced a series of pistols designed by Ferdinand Mannlicher for the commercial market, and these enjoyed a wide sale. It was hoped that a development of these handguns might eventually be adopted

as a military sidearm, but it was not to be, although they were bought privately and proved very popular with army officers.

Subsequent pistols that were manufactured at the factory were more successful with the military authorities, who adopted a Roth-Steyr model for the Austro-Hungarian armies in 1907. These weapons continued to be produced until 1912, when the design was replaced by another Steyr-built model. During World War I, the number of workers employed at the Steyr plant rose to 14,000, a figure that included many prisoners of war. Production output at that period achieved record proportions, with more than five million rifles and nearly 235,000 pistols being manufactured.

In 1934 the company merged with the Daimler-Puch concern and assumed the new title of Steyr-Daimler-Puch AG. By the year 1939, however, German troops had occupied the country and the factory was placed under the control of the Wehrmacht, who authorized it to be renamed as the Herman-Goeringwerke. Thereafter, huge quantities of arms were produced for the German war effort, which also included the manufacture of aircraft engines for the Luftwaffe. At the end of World War II the factory came under the occupation of the Russian army, and after this the American military authorities took over the administrating power when Austria was divided into four occupied zones.

## Detail Information for the Steyr 9mm Repetierpistole M12

The 9mm Steyr pistol was developed at the Austrian Arms Factory during the year 1910 as a progression of the Model 7 system Roth pistol, which it ultimately replaced as a military weapon. Much of the design for both weapons is credited to Karel Krnka. In order to distinguish the M12 more readily from the previous striker-fired

## Specifications for the Steyr Model 1912 Repetierpistole M12
**System:** Locked breech, recoil operated
**Calibre:** 9mm
**Pistol length:** 216mm
**Barrel length:** 130mm
**Grooves:** Four RH twist
**Magazine:** Eight rounds
**Weight (empty):** 990g
**Weight (loaded):** 1,086g
**Safety:** Thumb lever

model, the new pistol became known colloquially as the Steyr Hahn, or hammer version. While there were obvious differences in construction, both weapons utilized a similar type of locking arrangement, in which the barrel was rotated during the recoil action to disengage from the breech.

The first military series of the new pistol was exported to Chile in South America before World War I. Larger quantities were also purchased by the Rumanian military shortly afterwards, and other European countries began to show interest in the weapon. Following the declaration of war by Austro-Hungaria against Serbia in June 1914, the output of military weapons became a matter of the utmost urgency and production of the pistol was dramatically increased. By September 1914 orders had been received from the Imperial War Ministry to commence large-scale manufacture of the 9mm pistol for the Austrian army. At least 290,000 were produced before the Armistice of 1918, when serial manufacture was terminated.

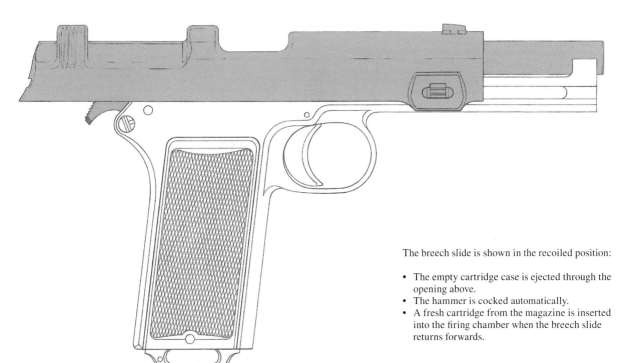

The breech slide is shown in the recoiled position:

- The empty cartridge case is ejected through the opening above.
- The hammer is cocked automatically.
- A fresh cartridge from the magazine is inserted into the firing chamber when the breech slide returns forwards.

Under the terms of the Versailles Treaty the factory was forbidden to engage in further production of military weapons, although the M12 pistol remained in service as an official sidearm of the Austrian Federal Army and the State Police until 1938. Additional supplies had been stored in Austrian government arsenals, where they remained until the country was annexed by the Nazis as part of the new German Reich. All weapons were then confiscated by the Wehrmacht, who converted the pistol to accept the standard German Parabellum cartridge.

The Steyr Model 1912 is a locked breech pistol and is formed with a series of projections on the barrel to facilitate the unlocking procedure. There are two lugs on the top surface that engage with two grooves on the inner face of the breech slide, while the unlocking action is controlled by a spiral rib on the lower surface of the barrel running in a helical groove on the pistol body to give a twisting motion. An additional lug acts as a stop for the backward motion of the barrel as the breech recoils after the weapon is fired.

**The breech slide assembly:** Contains an extractor, and the firing pin with spring, and is secured at the front of the pistol body by a transverse steel wedge, which also acts on the recoil spring.

**The recoil spring:** Lies beneath the barrel with a small guide cap at each end. The front cap bears against the wedge, while the rear cap rests against the trigger to provide it with spring action.

**The magazine:** Formed as part of the pistol grip, and is not detachable. When the breech is opened, cartridges are fed into the magazine reservoir from an eight-round charger. Cartridges may also be fed singly. At the left side of the pistol body, immedi-ately above the grip plate, is a cartridge release catch that can be manually depressed in order to empty the magazine of its contents through an open breech.

**Safety lever:** Also mounted on the rear left side of the pistol body, where it can be moved upwards to engage notches cut under the breech slide and simultaneously block forward movement of the hammer. In this state the weapon cannot be fired.

**Grip plates:** Normally of walnut and secured by a single screw at the lower left side of the pistol. Removal of the screw permits both grip plates to be withdrawn, and also allows the magazine base assembly to be removed.

**The firing mechanism:** External hammer and internal firing pin.

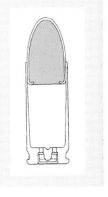

## Cartridge Information
Details for the 9mm Steyr cartridge:

**Bullet weight:** 7.5g
**Bullet diameter:** 9.02mm
**Bullet length:** 15.1mm
**Case length:** 23.1mm
**Rim diameter:** 9.65mm
**Cartridge length:** 32.95mm
**Cartridge weight:** 12g
**Initial velocity:** 360m/s

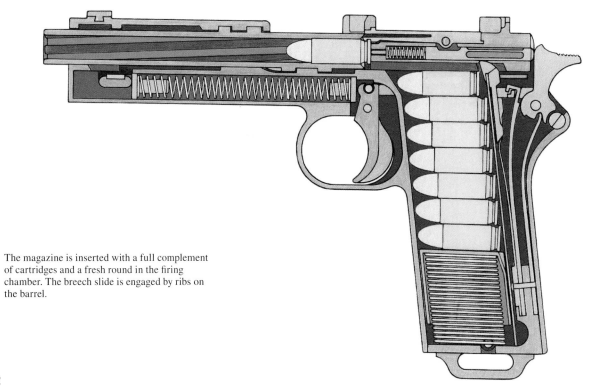

The magazine is inserted with a full complement of cartridges and a fresh round in the firing chamber. The breech slide is engaged by ribs on the barrel.

# 17 Tokarev Model 1930 (Russia)

## *Pistolet TT30 (7.62mm Model 1930)*

### *Regulation sidearm of the Russian military forces in World War II*

**Factory: Tula Arms Factory, Tula, Russia**

An arms factory was initially established at Tula, Russia, on 15 February 1712 by order of the Emperor Peter I. Two further workshops were erected in 1714, and special tools were installed to accelerate production. The eighteenth century was a period of highly artistic employment for Russian gunmakers, most of whom were specialists in many forms of ornate work on sporting weapons. In the early part of the next century, involvement in warfare had required the purchase of foreign-made weapons for the imperial army, and it became necessary to increase Russian manufacturing capabilities.

By 1885, arrangements had been made for American Smith & Wesson revolvers to be constructed, and this led to the installation of new mass-production machinery at the factory, followed by a vast programme of expansion to cope with the increased demand for infantry rifles. More than 8,000 workers were employed at that time, and military weapons were produced on a large scale. In the development of small arms, the factory also engaged several notable Russian arms designers, including Sergei Mosin, creator of the first Russian rifle, Vasily Degtyarev, designer of the first Russian machinegun, and Theodore Tokarev, who produced a self-loading pistol.

Production facilities at Tula continued to increase during the twentieth century as a result of the two World Wars, with weapons of all types being manufactured. The factory was able to produce modified versions of the Maxim machinegun for the army, and created a weapon that enjoyed a long production run.

Soviet Russia, in common with several other European countries involved in the conflict of 1939–45, was not fully prepared for war, but within a remarkably short period had developed weapons that were at least equal to those of opposing forces. A salient feature of all Russian weapons produced at that period was that they could be manufactured and assembled by semi-skilled labour on machinery of maximum tolerances. The Tula-Tokarev self-loading pistols in particular were greatly simplified in their construction to permit easier manufacture, and so continued to be produced for almost twenty years, becoming one of the most robust and reliable of all military handguns.

In addition to his pistol design, Tokarev was also responsible for the creation of other weapons, notably the first automatic rifle to be adopted by the Soviet armed forces. Vast quantities of all automatic weapons were produced at Tula for the Great Patriotic War.

## Detail Information for the Tokarev 7.62mm Pistolet Tulski Tokarev Abrazyets 1930/33

Acknowledged as the first locked breech automatic pistol to be adopted by the Russian army, the Tokarev model bears the name of its designer, Theodore Tokarev, a senior technician at the State Arms Plant in Tula. The original model was created in 1929 and underwent tests by the Soviet War Committee in the following year. It was basically a modified version of the Browning design, with locking ribs around the barrel engaging with corresponding grooves machined from inside the breech slide, plus a swinging link for disengagement.

Designed specifically for military purposes and mass production, the pistol was relatively simple in construction. Its main feature was a detachable sub-frame containing the hammer,

**Specifications for the Tokarev Model 1930 Pistolet TT30**
**System:** Locked breech, recoil operated
**Calibre:** 7.62mm
**Pistol length:** 195mm
**Barrel length:** 117mm
**Grooves:** Four RH twist
**Magazine:** Eight rounds
**Weight (empty):** 854g
**Weight (loaded):** 940g
**Safety:** None

mainspring and sear, all of which could be easily removed for maintenance. Two arms extending from each side of the housing serve as guides for feeding cartridges into the firing chamber. In contrast to most military automatic pistols, there is no manually operated safety device, but merely a half-cock notch on the hammer to prevent it from being fired.

The Tokarev pistol was first used in combat by Russian troops after May 1939 during the Russo-Japanese campaigns on the Manchurian border, and again in the Soviet invasion of Finland in the winter of 1939–40. It was then employed in the Great Patriotic War, and in Korea from 1950 to 1953. Production at Tula had commenced in 1930, though fewer than 5,000 pistols were manufactured before a second version of the original model was introduced in 1933. The main improvement concerned a change to the locking ribs on the barrel, while only minor alterations were made to other components. During World War II, pistols made by factories other than at Tula were fitted with walnut

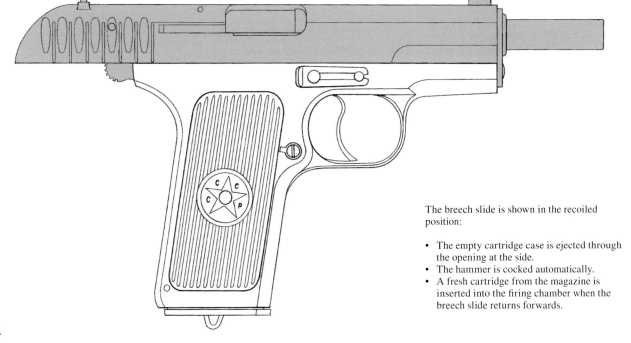

The breech slide is shown in the recoiled position:

- The empty cartridge case is ejected through the opening at the side.
- The hammer is cocked automatically.
- A fresh cartridge from the magazine is inserted into the firing chamber when the breech slide returns forwards.

grip plates rather than the usual black plastic material. When the German army invaded Russia, captured examples of the Tokarev pistol received a new title of Pistole 615(r) and were adapted to fire Mauser 7.63 cartridges. For experimental purposes, other models were even converted to fire the standard German 9mm cartridge.

Russian manufacture of the pistol continued for a brief period after the war when other Communist satellite countries were encouraged to adopt the design. After 1948, manufacture of the pistol began at the National Manufacturing Plant at Budapest in Hungary. Although it was originally identical to the Russian example, that particular model was later revised in 1958 to accept the 9mm Parabellum cartridge, and was furnished with a new safety device.

By the year 1949, the weapon had become obsolete as a Soviet military sidearm and its production in Russia was discontinued. Many thousands of the Tokarev pistol were then produced throughout the 1950s by various Communist countries, including Poland, Yugoslavia and China. The pistol was used by Chinese troops during the Korean War with the title of Type 51 or Type 54, although they were very similar to the post-war Russian pistols.

**The breech slide:** Contains an extractor, firing pin and spring. A barrel bushing is fitted at the front end of the breech slide, and has an extension drilled to accept the front guide for the recoil spring.

**The barrel:** Reinforced at the chamber end, and has a forked portion to accommodate the swinging link. There are two circular locking ribs around the barrel for engagement with the breech slide. The front end of the barrel fits into the barrel bushing.

**The recoil spring:** Has a small guide at the front end and lies in an open channel on the pistol body, where it is compressed between the barrel bushing and a longer spring guide at the rear.

**The grip plates:** Of black synthetic material with vertical ribs and a central star motif. Each plate is held to the grip by an internal locking latch, which is accessible when the magazine is removed.

## Cartridge Information

Details for the 7.62mm Tokarev cartridge:

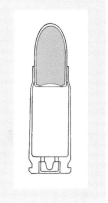

**Bullet weight:** 5.5g
**Bullet diameter:** 7.87mm
**Bullet length:** 14.3mm
**Case length:** 24.6mm
**Rim diameter:** 9.9mm
**Cartridge length:** 34.5mm
**Cartridge weight:** 10.2g
**Initial velocity:** 455m/s

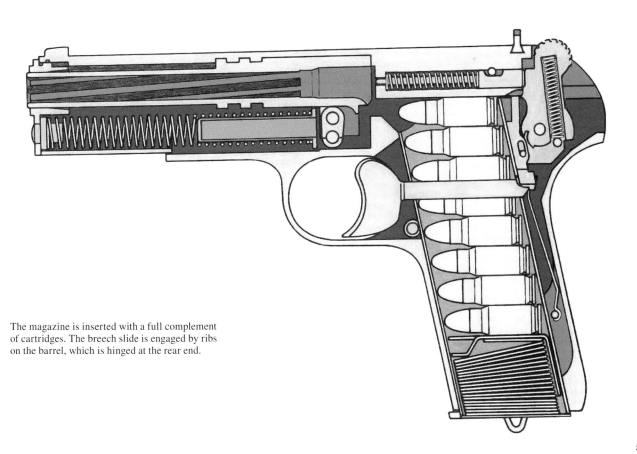

The magazine is inserted with a full complement of cartridges. The breech slide is engaged by ribs on the barrel, which is hinged at the rear end.

# 18 Walther Model 1938 (Germany)

## *Pistole P38 (9mm Model 1938)*

*Regulation sidearm of the German military forces in World War II*

**Factory: Waffenfabrik Walther,
Zella-Mehlis, Germany**

The origins of the Walther factory can be traced back to 1886, when Carl Walther set up a small workshop in the small town of Zella Sankt Blasii for the manufacture of target rifles. He rapidly gained a reputation for the high quality of his work, and the business expanded as a family concern throughout the following years, with the construction of larger factory premises to include the production of a wide variety of self-loading pistols. After the death of Carl Walther in 1915, the responsibility of managing the firm rested with his three sons, Fritz, Georg and Erich. Being the eldest, Fritz Walther became the senior partner in control of the business, which by then was fully engaged with the avaricious demands of war. It was Fritz Walther who was responsible for the pistol designs, many of which were adopted officially by the military and various police authorities.

The popular Walther Model 4 pistol was produced in large numbers as a sidearm for German officers during World War I. Production facilities were, of necessity, considerably streamlined at that time, without detracting from the quality of the products, and further new buildings were constructed in order to cope with the vast increase in orders from the armed forces.

When the war ended in November 1918, all arms manufacture was brought to a complete halt and the Walther management were faced with the immediate dilemma of providing a new use for their technicians and machinery. At first the factory turned to the manufacture of optical parts merely to retain and occupy their technical staff, but by the year 1920, it was possible to resume the production of sporting arms and small calibre pistols. In the meantime, the original name for the factory location was changed from Zella Sankt Blasii to Zella-Mehlis, because of the incorporation of another local township. Other pistol models in various calibres were gradually added to the factory output by the 1930s to include the successful PP and PPK Models. This was followed by the introduction of a new, locked breech military pistol in 1937, and this heralded an era of prosperity for the firm, with that weapon being mass produced as the P38 for the German military.

By 1939 the Walther company had become one of the most important industrial firms in the region, with more than 2,000 people employed in its several plants. Most of the factory buildings were demolished during World War II, but the Walther firm emerged again to continue its business at Ulm.

## Detail Information for the Walther 9mm Pistole P38

This pistol was conceived in the years immediately prior to World War II as a progressive development of a Walther police model but for military use. Its locked breech design had been patented in 1936, with contributions by Fritz Walther and Fritz Barthelmes. A prototype was then submitted to the German military authorities for testing in 1937, and this was eventually adopted as an official regulation weapon in 1938 to replace the current Luger model. Following its adoption, the pistol was also accepted as a standard

**Specifications for the Walther Model 1938 Pistole P38**
**System:** Locked breech, recoil operated
**Calibre:** 9mm
**Pistol length:** 214mm
**Barrel length:** 125mm
**Grooves:** Six RH twist
**Magazine:** Eight rounds
**Weight (empty):** 780g
**Weight (loaded):** 878g
**Safety:** Thumb lever

sidearm of the Swedish forces one year later. Known initially as the Heeres Pistole (army pistol), it was introduced as the Walther HP model; its construction made extensive use of stamped components instead of machined parts, and it was therefore cheaper to manufacture. Design of the early examples differed from the adopted P38 model in having an enclosed hammer, which did not meet with military approval. It has been estimated that approximately 25,000 of the HP model were produced before the beginning of World War II. Production then concentrated on the adopted military version to satisfy the demands of the German war effort.

In addition to those pistols manufactured by Walther, production was also undertaken by various other arms factories, including the giant Mauser plant at Oberndorf, where more than 320,000 pistols were manufactured in order to maintain supplies. A further 280,000 were also produced by the Spreewerke factory

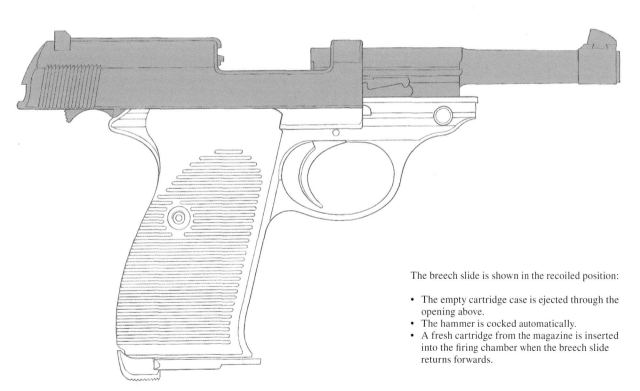

The breech slide is shown in the recoiled position:

- The empty cartridge case is ejected through the opening above.
- The hammer is cocked automatically.
- A fresh cartridge from the magazine is inserted into the firing chamber when the breech slide returns forwards.

in Berlin during the war period, bringing a total of well over 1,200,000 pistols delivered to the German armed forces by all the factories engaged in its production. After 1945, some manufacture was even undertaken at Oberndorf by the French authorities. Output of the P38 model was resumed at the Walther Ulm factory in 1957, with the manufacture of new lightweight pistols of aluminium alloy for the West German Bundeswehr.

The firing mechanism of the P38 differed from most automatic pistols in being a double-action system, which did not require the initial cocking of the hammer to be achieved by breech action. The Walther pistol is also unusual in its breech-locking arrangement by having a hinged locking block within the barrel extension to release engagement from the breech after the weapon is fired. Another useful feature is the provision of a cartridge indicator.

**The breech slide:** Contains the extractor, and the firing pin and its spring, together with a loaded chamber indicator and spring. Components of the safety assembly are also fitted in the rear section, while a large upper front portion of the breech slide is cut away to provide a satisfactory ejection of spent cartridge cases.

**The barrel:** Formed with a special housing at its rear portion to contain elements of the locking mechanism. A small lever at the forward left side of the pistol body can be operated to release the barrel together with the breech slide from the pistol assembly.

**The recoil springs:** Of small diameter and arranged within channels at each side of the pistol body. A long rod is provided at the front of each spring to serve as a guide during compression.

**The safety lever:** Conveniently positioned at the rear left side of the breech slide, and is operated to block the firing pin, thus enabling the weapon to be carried with a live round in the chamber and the hammer down without fear of accidental discharge.

**The magazine:** Retained in the grip by a spring-operated catch at the rear of the butt, and released by moving the catch back.

**The grip plates:** Normally of wood with a pattern of vertical grooves, and secured by a single screw at the left side entering a nut at the opposite side. There is a moulded depression at the base of the left-hand plate with an opening to receive a lanyard loop. Commercial examples had plates made of a synthetic material.

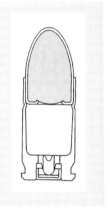

### Cartridge Information
Details for the 9mm Parabellum cartridge:

**Bullet weight:** 8g
**Bullet diameter:** 9.02mm
**Bullet length:** 15.25mm
**Case length:** 19.3mm
**Rim diameter:** 9.96mm
**Cartridge length:** 29.2mm
**Cartridge weight:** 12.1g
**Initial velocity:** 345m/s

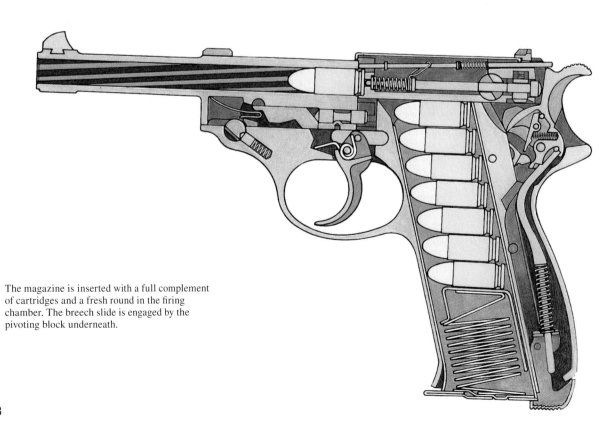

The magazine is inserted with a full complement of cartridges and a fresh round in the firing chamber. The breech slide is engaged by the pivoting block underneath.

# 19 Webley Model 1912 (Britain)

## *Pistol self-loading .455 Mk. I (.455 Model 1912)*

*Regulation sidearm of the British military forces in World War I*

**Factory: Webley & Scott Limited, Birmingham, England**

In 1835, the brothers Philip and James Webley traded as makers of percussion revolvers in Birmingham, while the firm of W&C Scott & Son was involved with the manufacture of rifles. After the death of James Webley in 1856, the administration of their gun-making business passed to Philip Webley, who continued to promote the manufacture of revolvers. By the year 1870 he had been joined by his two sons to form the company Philip Webley & Son, and proceeded to secure many important contracts for the supply of weapons. A turning point in the company history came in July 1887 with an order from the British War Office for thousands of service revolvers.

Philip Webley died on 24 March 1888, leaving his sons Thomas and Henry in control of the business, which continued to expand with ever-increasing sales of revolvers. By amalgamating with other Birmingham gunmakers on 21 October 1897, P. Webley & Son became the Webley & Scott Revolver and Arms Company Limited. Although primarily concerned with the design and manufacture of revolvers, it was not long before an interest in automatic weapons was aroused. The first weapon in this category

was a Mars self-loading pistol, but it proved too cumbersome to operate and so was not made commercially.

A more successful design appeared in 1901, in the form of an automatic revolver capable of firing British Service ammunition. However, although it functioned well and was sold commercially, it was never officially adopted by the military authorities, who preferred to continue acquiring large quantities of regular Webley revolvers. Production of automatic pistols commenced in 1905, with a patented design created by William Whiting, managing director at the Birmingham factory. Developments of that weapon were produced in quantity for the British police, and eventually led to a series of larger military versions.

During World War I, the company was placed under contract to provide service revolvers for the British government, and this resulted in a complete halt to further production for the private sector. A new factory was then completed at the same site in Birmingham for the increased wartime demand. With the inevitable decline in arms manufacture throughout the interwar period, the company chose to diversify and turned its attention to the introduction of air pistols in 1924. In the meantime it had been commissioned to prepare designs for a new service revolver, and was successful by 1926. The demand for weapons continued when war broke out in 1939.

## Detail Information for the Webley & Scott Pistol Self-loading .455in Mk. I

This Webley was the first automatic pistol to be officially adopted for service with the British armed forces. It was designed and subsequently patented in 1906 by William Whiting, who would be responsible for the creation of several other automatic pistols for the Webley & Scott Company. The pistol was produced in two

**Specifications for the Webley Model 1912 Pistol Self-loading .455 Mk. I**
**System:** Locked breech, recoil operated
**Calibre:** 11.6mm
**Pistol length:** 216mm
**Barrel length:** 127mm
**Grooves:** Six RH twist
**Magazine:** Seven rounds
**Weight (empty):** 1,106g
**Weight (loaded):** 1,253g
**Safety:** Grip lever

types, one known as the navy pattern and the other as an army version, which later became known as the RHA model after it was adopted for use by regiments of the Royal Horse Artillery. The calibre 455in model had been intended purely as a military weapon, and was first submitted for firing trials by the British War Office in 1905, although the results were inconclusive. Tests by the navy did not take place until 1909, by which time the new pistol had been greeted with more enthusiasm and was considered to be superior to the existing service revolver. Further testing continued before the British Admiralty eventually confirmed the adoption of the pistol in February 1912, but in limited quantities: by the end of 1917 just over 7,600 had been delivered. In addition to the Admiralty contract, during 1913 more than 500 examples were also dispatched to the Australian government.

The RHA model adopted for land service was similar in construction to the navy pistol, but featured an adjustable rear sight and detachable shoulder stock. It was officially approved

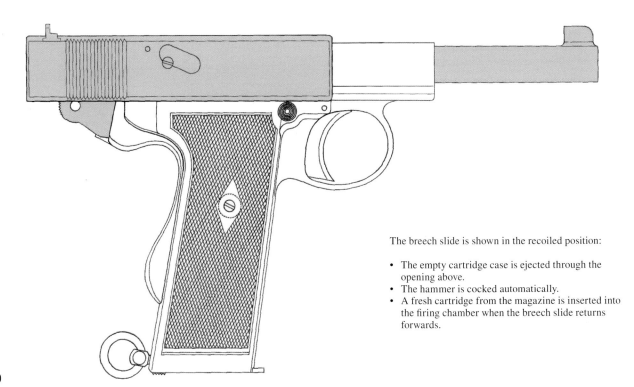

The breech slide is shown in the recoiled position:

- The empty cartridge case is ejected through the opening above.
- The hammer is cocked automatically.
- A fresh cartridge from the magazine is inserted into the firing chamber when the breech slide returns forwards.

for issue to all branches of the British armed forces in April 1915. As with the case of navy contracts, quantities of this model were also limited, and by the end of 1919 fewer than 440 had been supplied under contract for the government. While the Webley & Scott Company had been undecided about entering the commercial market with such a large calibre weapon, manufacture of the automatic pistol for private sales proceeded until the end of 1916 and was then resumed after World War I, ending with a production total of 1,259.

The breech-locking system of this pistol is unique in employing a set of inclined projections on the barrel to lower it from engagement with the breech after the weapon is fired. This form of construction required close-tolerance machining, and was therefore susceptible to problems caused by dirt entering the mechanism. The Webley & Scott .455 model has the distinction of being the first and only British automatic pistol to be accepted for military use. Many were purchased privately by army officers during World War I, although the regulation sidearm was then a revolver of the same calibre. The last model was produced by the Birmingham factory at the end of December 1933.

**The breech slide:** Contains the extractor, firing pin and spring. It is short and does not completely cover the barrel. Diagonal grooves are machined from both inner faces of the breech slide to match projections on the barrel and keep both items locked together.

**The barrel:** Formed with a large rear extension of rectangular section, which is machined with two sloping projections at each side for a locking engagement with the breech slide.

**The recoil spring:** A flat, laminar V-spring acting in combination with a long lever to re-close the breech following each discharge.

**The safety lever:** Fitted to the rear of the grip, and operated when grasping the pistol to move the sear into contact with the trigger bar, thus connecting the firing mechanism.

**The magazine:** Retained within the grip by a spring-operated catch at the lower rear edge. There are two notches in the magazine for engagement of the catch, one for repeated shooting, the other for single shots, with rounds fed from above the breech.

**The grip plates:** Made of a hardened rubber compound (vulcanite), and cut with a fine chequered pattern; each plate is secured to the grip by a single screw at the centre.

### Cartridge Information
Details for the 455in Webley cartridge:

**Bullet weight:** 14.5g
**Bullet diameter:** 11.5mm
**Bullet length:** 15mm
**Case length:** 23.7mm
**Rim diameter:** 12.8mm
**Cartridge length:** 31.2mm
**Cartridge weight:** 21g
**Initial velocity:** 229m/s, 700fps

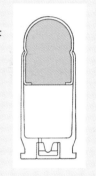

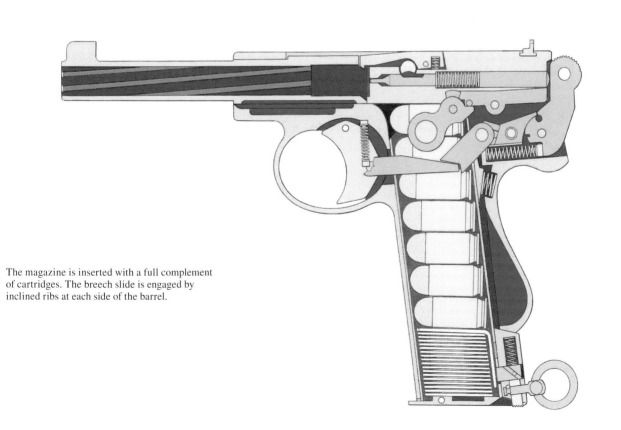

The magazine is inserted with a full complement of cartridges. The breech slide is engaged by inclined ribs at each side of the barrel.

# Operation of the Semi-Automatic Pistol

Strictly speaking, the term 'automatic pistol' is not entirely acceptable, as it tends to imply that the weapon is used as a machine gun. Therefore, it has become generally more appropriate for the description of 'semi-automatic' or 'self-loading pistol' to be applied.

While the standard revolver is capable of presenting a fresh cartridge for each pull of the trigger, it has no means for automatically ejecting the spent casings, and single action shooting also requires the hammer to be cocked manually. In a semi-automatic pistol, the system permits rounds to be fed from a magazine containing more ammunition and, after each shot, the spent casing is ejected automatically and the firing mechanism is set at full cock for the next shot.

There are two types of system, blowback and locked breech.

## Blowback

The action relies solely on the principle of a strong recoil spring to hold the breech closed as the weapon is fired. This method is normally sufficient to keep the breech safely closed until the bullet has passed through the barrel.

## Locked Breech

This system is required when shooting cartridges of greater power. The barrel is secured to the breech unit when firing takes place and so both units initially recoil together. When the bullet has left the barrel, the latter is halted and is disconnected from the breech unit, which continues to move back against pressure from a recoil spring. It is then forced forwards again by the spring action to re-engage with the barrel. As it does so, a fresh cartridge is moved up from the magazine to be pushed into the firing chamber by the returning breech unit.

## Firing System

There are two types of firing system:

- In which a cocked striker pin is held against the pressure of a spring and released by trigger operation to discharge the cartridge.
- In which a hammer is employed to be operated by the trigger for striking the firing pin and igniting the cartridge.

When the weapon is fired, the cartridge primer cap is struck and ignites to explode the powder and generate the pressure to expel the bullet. At the same instant, the pressure also creates a recoil movement of the cartridge case against the breech face, thus forcing the breech back to an 'open' position.

## Ejection

When the breech is fully open, an extractor claw fitted to the breech unit pulls against the cartridge rim to flip the spent casing through the breech opening.

## Rifling

The barrel bore is cut with a series of spiral grooves to create a turning motion of the bullet as it passes through the bore. This produces better accuracy of the projectile on its way to the target.

## Disconnection

Most pistols employ a mechanism to prevent more than one shot to be made when pulling the trigger. This consists of a device operated during breech recoil to break the connection between the trigger and striker unit. The system is restored when the trigger pressure is released, thus enabling a second shot to be achieved. Without a disconnector, the pistol would continue to fire further rounds from the magazine until finger pressure on the trigger is released.

## THE EUROPA MILITARIA SERIES

Full-colour photographic paperback reference books on the armies of today and yesterday, for collectors, modellers, re-enactors, wargamers, illustrators, and military history students of all kinds.
All 64 pages, 260 × 190mm.

EM No. 6: Waffen-SS Uniforms in Colour Photos

EM No. 17: Wehrmacht Camouflage Uniforms & Post-War Derivatives

EM No. 18: Waffen-SS Camouflage Uniforms & Post-War Derivatives

EM No. 20: The Guards: Britain's Household Division

EM No. 25: Warrior Company

EM No. 32: British Web Equipment of the Two World Wars

EM No. 33: American Web Equipment 1910–1967

EM No. 34: British Post-War Jungle Webbing

EM No. 35: Modern British Webbing Equipment

EM No. 36: Warsaw Pact Badges

EM No. 37: American Web Equipment 1967–1991

EM No. 38: British Military Respirators and Anti-Gas Equipment of the Two World Wars

## EUROPA MILITARIA SPECIALS

All titles 96 pages, 260 × 190mm.

EMS No. 2: The Roman Legions Recreated in Colour Photos

EMS No. 6: The Vikings

EMS No. 7: World War II British Women's Uniforms

EMS No. 8: Medieval Military Costume

EMS No. 11: Napoleon's Line Infantry & Artillery Recreated in Colour Photos

EMS No. 12: Napoleon's Imperial Guard Recreated in Colour Photos

EMS No. 14: The Samurai

EMS No. 16: Confederate Troops of the American Civil War

EMS No. 17: Union Troops of the American Civil War

EMS No. 18: The Medieval Fighting Man: Costume and Equipment 800–1500

In case of difficulty in ordering, please contact the sales office:

The Crowood Press Ltd
Ramsbury
Wiltshire
SN8 2HR
UK

Tel: 44 (0) 1672 520320

enquiries@crowood.com

www.crowood.com